ON BELAY

72 Daily Meditations
for Adults and Adolescents

ON BELAY

72 Daily Meditations
for Adults and Adolescents

Patricia M.B. Kitchen
Crawford F. Brubaker III

KALEIDOSCOPE PUBLISHING
PHILADELPHIA, PENNSYLVANIA

Printed in the United States of America.

No part of this book may be reproduced or transmitted in any form or by any means, electronic or mechanical, including photocopying, recording, or by any information storage and retrieval system, without written permission from the publisher. For information, address Kaleidoscope Publishing, 295 E. Swedesford Road, #121, Wayne, Pennsylvania, 19087. To obtain more copies of this book, address P.M.B.K, 625 Montgomery Avenue, Bryn Mawr, Pennsylvania, 19010.

ISBN 0-9706593-9-3

Scripture quotations, unless otherwise noted, are from the New Revised Standard Version of the Bible, copyrighted © 1989 by the Division of Christian Education of the National Council of the Churches of Christ in the United States of America, and are used by permission. Owing to limitations of space, all other permissions and acknowledgements regarding previously published material will be found on pages 175 and 176.

First edition published by
KALEIDOSCOPE PUBLISHING
610.962.0208
KScopePub@aol.com • www.kaleidoscopepublishing.com

WRITTEN AND EDITED WITH GRATITUDE TO:

The North Carolina Outward Bound School,
Asheville, North Carolina

and

The Ropes Course Program of The Lawrenceville School
Lawrenceville, New Jersey

. . . who have helped define,
through extraordinary experiences,
the term "on belay" for us.

Contents

INTRODUCTION

THEIR VOICES echoed in the canyon, "On belay!" and then before long, "Off belay!" The odd phrase was repeated throughout the afternoon by people climbing and rapelling all around us, like Daddy-Long-Legs down a wall. In the vicinity there were a parent and teen, fraternity brothers, and a group of lively women. It was our first experience with carabeners, multi-colored climbing ropes, and harnesses, but by the time the sun was starting to slip over the shoulder of the mountain, we understood what "on belay" meant.

We understood that the risk of rock climbing requires dependable partners. Experienced climbers will tell you it is foolhardy to climb alone. While climbing across the Blue Ridge or Rocky Mountains calls for the physical presence of another, climbing through the rocky terrain of everyday life calls for the presence of God. Daily, we can be "on belay" with God. We do so through prayer, Bible or Torah readings, and through authentic connections with friends who are fellow seekers. Crawford and I have come to realize that a parent and teenager can also be on belay with one another. And need to be so. Strength is shared. Tough decisions are negotiated. Trust is in place. As the wild winds of adolescence blow at gale force, parents and teens need, more than ever, to be on belay with one another.

This small book is intended for fellow climbers and friends of diverse faiths. It is for people who look out at the world and see a spiritual landscape where compassion toward nature and each other must prevail. And it is for those who look within themselves and see a broad frontier, and feel it is time to explore its terrain.

The experience of being "on belay" with God is usually strengthened during Sabbath time. Whether this time falls every Sunday or from sundown Friday to sunset Saturday, at sunrise each day, or each evening just before your lamp is turned off, God's presence can penetrate our lives and move into focus. The Sabbath journey can begin in prayer and meditation, apart from the whir and responsibilities of daily life. This Sabbath time, a holy time of rest and reflection, replenishes our spirits through the mystery of God's calming, *sometimes startling,* presence. We need that which is *holy* in our lives. And we need *each other.*

In his book *The Birth of God,* John B. Rogers, Jr. speaks of "the encompassing mystery which graciously upholds and sustains us." Picture the thread of divine mystery, that which both tugs and supports us, as being "on belay" with God. Rogers writes: "In our time, faith, hope and love are beset by pain and violence. To live by faith may not mean less pain or less distress; the way of faith is not a detour around adversity. Indeed, there are circumstances in which faith seems only to sustain us, to help us endure. Sometimes we can do no more than cling to the faith of others. Sometimes the faith of the church [or synagogue], locally and historically, has to bear us along in our doubt and disability. . . . 'There are times when I just cannot say the creed,' said one of my parishioners. 'I'll say it for you until you can say it again,' I replied. 'Whether or not you were aware of it, there have been times when you have had to say it for me; and I shall probably need you to do so again in the future.' "

When pain or fear knocks at the door of a teenager's life, dependable friends are crucial, but a steady parent, offering unconditional love, is irreplaceable: a compass to steer us when we cannot tell North from South; a light to guide us when we are lost in relentless darkness; and the wind which blows us home. Having a parent or significant adult to rely upon is a huge asset through the rocky years of being a teenager. Often, as teenagers, we crave independence and freedom suddenly and inexplicably. No sooner do we celebrate our thirteenth birthdays than we are on to adventure and experimentation. At times, dangerous temptations can loom upon us. We do not want to be held back but our parents love us too much to let us go completely. A tough tether remains intact; a climbing rope holds for when the slope is most slippery. They know the rough edges of the world, and how deeply those edges can cut. Their paternal fibers instinctively want to weave a net of protection around us to prevent overexposure to a world laced with greed, lust, selfishness, and unhealthy temptation. We need lifegiving connections of trust at any age, but perhaps more acutely as adolescents and parents.

May these meditations breathe hope into your bones as we live "on belay" with one another.

August 16, 2000, Pocono Lake, Pennsylvania

On Belay

72 Daily Meditations
for Adults and Adolescents

PART I

Internal Compass

"Let's start out all over again"

"For behold, I create new heavens and a new earth; and the former things shall not be remembered or come to mind. But be glad and rejoice forever in what I create; for behold, I create Jerusalem for rejoicing, and her people for gladness. I will also rejoice in Jerusalem, and be glad in My people; and there will no longer be heard in her the voice of weeping and the sound of crying."
Isaiah 65:17-19

"I have wiped out your transgressions like a thick cloud, and your sins like a heavy mist. Return to Me, for I have redeemed you."
Isaiah 44:22

THE HARVARD DOCTOR and professor, Robert Coles, has done extensive work with children, including research on the development of their spiritual and moral landscape. He tells of an event one morning in Boston when he was working as a volunteer fourth-grade teacher in an inner-city elementary school. Dr. Coles, a wise and gentle man, describes weeks of disorder in the classroom as he tried to engage these challenging children. He writes, "One morning, however, the limits of my patience were stretched too far. Suddenly, I lost my cool; I abandoned my rational efforts at persuasion in favor of – well, an outburst. I picked up the blackboard pointer, slammed it down on the desk, shouted a loud NO at the entire class, and then told them off. I said I was through putting up with their rudeness and that if they didn't shape up, I simply wouldn't come back. When I finished talking I noticed something: an almost eerie silence that, in fact lasted – thereby challenging me to respond. I now spoke in a more subdued tone, but was still upset, and I wanted the children to hear why. My explanation was followed by another spell of silence – and I doubt I'll ever forget a girl's comment that broke the ice: 'Let's start out all over again.' "

As a child I loved the Etch-A-Sketch we had among our toys. I would get lost in a world of fine lines that intertwined in fanciful patterns, created simply by the turning of two knobs on opposite sides of the red frame. And then, when the picture reached a point of chaos, too many lines and the pattern obscured, I was fascinated with the capacity to simply shake the toy and make a clean screen emerge. For me, and I wonder if it is so for you, there is something therapeutic, mystical, and surely hopeful, about a clean slate. The sense of starting out all over again. When a child shakes an Etch-A-Sketch and produces a clean surface, she is ready to begin again . . . to re-create. This is a simplistic illustration but one which shares a holy base with the God of Israel; the God of you and me.

From "They Did Not Know How to Blush," Patricia M.B. Kitchen and *Harvard Diary II: Essays on the Sacred and the Secular,* by Dr. Robert Coles

---

I believe, O Lord, that your love for me is new every morning, yet some days I awaken feeling stale and unlovable. Wipe the slate of my life clean this day, I pray. Cleanse my intentions and my actions. And help me to make amends where I have caused harm. Renew my faith in your life-changing love from this point forward. Amen.

"I took the one less traveled by"

"Trust in the Lord with all your heart
And lean not on your own understanding
In all thy ways acknowledge Him
And He shall direct thy path."

Proverbs 3:5-6

The Road Not Taken

Two roads diverged in a yellow wood,
And sorry I could not travel both
And be one traveler; long I stood
And looked down one as far as I could
To where it bent in the undergrowth;

Then took the other, as just as fair,
And having perhaps the better claim,
Because it was grassy and wanted wear
Though as for that, the passing there
Had worn them really about the same.

And both that morning equally lay,
In leaves no step had trodden black.
Oh, I kept the first for another day!
Yet knowing how way leads on to way,
I doubted if I should ever come back.

I shall be telling this with a sigh

Somewhere ages and ages hence;
Two roads diverged in a wood, and I –
I took the one less traveled by,
And that has made all the difference.

Robert Frost (1874–1963)

My Lord God,
I have no idea where I am going.
I do not see the road ahead of me.
I cannot know for certain where it will end.
Nor do I really know myself,
    And the fact that I think that I am following Your will
        Does not mean that I am actually doing so.
But I believe that the desire to please You
                        does in fact please You.
And I hope that I have that desire in all that I am doing.
I hope that I will never do anything apart from that desire.
And I know that if I do this,
You will lead me by the right road
though I may know nothing about it.
Therefore will I trust You always
though I may seem to be lost and in the shadow of death.
I will not fear, for You are ever with me,
and You will never leave me to face my perils alone. Amen.

Thomas Merton (1915–1968)

"The North Star of my life"

"Now the Lord said to Abram, 'Go from your country and your kindred and your father's house to the land that I will show you. I will make of you a great nation, and I will bless you, and make your name great, so that you will be a blessing.' "

Genesis 12:1-2

Outward Bound

Where lies the land to which yon ship must go?
Fresh as a lark mounting at break of day
Festively she puts forth in trim array;
Is she for tropic suns, or polar snow?
What boots the inquiry? – Neither friend nor foe
She cares for; let her travel where she may,
She finds familiar names, a beaten way
Ever before her, and a wind to blow.
Yet still I ask, what haven is her mark?
And, almost as it was when ships were rare,
(From time to time, like pilgrims, here and there
Crossing the waters) doubt, and something dark,
Of the old sea some reverential fear,
Is with me at thy farewell, joyous bark!

William Wordsworth (1770–1850)

Be the North Star of my life, I pray, O Lord. Make partners of my curiosity and my courage and lead me on a journey of justice. Let the parameters of my life be as wide as your mercy, and the heights of my dreams as high as your great love. Amen.

4

"Dangerous dreams"

Thou hast turned for me my mourning into dancing.
Psalm 30:11

"See, I have set you this day over nations and over kingdoms,
To pluck up and to break down,
To destroy and to overthrow,
To build and to plant."
Jeremiah 1:10

THE DREAMS we harbor that long to sail like Clipper ships on open seas are, at times, fraught with daring and danger. Yet sometimes we hold quiet dreams, not dramatic ones, that still long to slip away from the dock of timidity and sail on a quieter lake. The prophet Jeremiah was commissioned "to pluck up and to pull down, to destroy and to overthrow," but he is also more gently encouraged "to build and to plant." But sometimes dreams, quiet or dangerous, are splintered, sometimes shattered. The building or planting we pour ourselves into is withered or destroyed.

In 1925, Karen Blixen, the Danish author of *Out of Africa*, left the bourgeois world of her family at age twenty-seven to embark upon a new life in Kenya on a coffee plantation. Her marriage was tepid. But her dreams of Africa were inexhaustible.

The farm failed, her marriage ended, and Karen was forced to return to Denmark. At this painful time she wrote these words to her mother:

"Dear Mother . . . You must not think that I feel, in spite of it having ended in such defeat, that my life has been wasted here, or that I would exchange it with that of anyone I know . . . For I have looked into the eyes of lions and slept under the Southern Cross, I have seen the grass of the great plains ablaze and covered with delicate green after the rains, I have been the friend of Somali, Kikuyu, and Masai, Oh, surely . . . I plucked the best rose of life!"

From "Dangerous Dreams," Patricia M.B. Kitchen

and *Between Ourselves: Letters Between Mothers and Daughters,* ed. Karen Payne

---

Dear God, take my world apart where rebuilding is needed. Reframe my life in your Divine image. May the windows of my soul be made clean again, and the rooms of my life be filled once again with light. Be my Foundation, I pray, this day and always. Amen.

5

"God answers in color"

Then God said to Noah and to his sons with him, "Behold I establish my covenant with you and your descendants after you, and with every living creature that is with you, the birds, the cattle, and every beast of the earth with you, as many as came out of the ark. I establish my covenant with you, that never again shall all flesh be cut off by the waters of a flood, and never again shall there be a flood to destroy the earth." And God said, "This is the sign of the covenant which I make between me and you and every living creature that is with you, for all future generations: I set my bow in the cloud, and it shall be a sign of the covenant between me and the earth. When I bring clouds over the earth and the bow is seen in the clouds, I will remember my covenant which is between me and you and every living creature of all flesh; and the waters shall never again become a flood to destroy all flesh."
Genesis 9:8-15

I SENSE THAT our tendency is to think and live in black and white. But God thinks, moves, and responds in color. When we ask tough black and white questions, or make hasty black and white judgments, God answers in color. Do you remember the first time you saw a prism create a rainbow of color? Or the first time you peered through a microscope?

A young musician I know wrote a song in which the phrase

"I'm looking for a rainbow in a black and white world . . ." caught my ear. It reminds me of how startled I felt as a child seeing Dorothy step out of the black and white cinematic world of Kansas and into the colorful outskirts of Oz. I would love to have been in the Hollywood conference room when that idea broke ground! Is it possible that our black and white mindset is a barrier to the deep, multi-colored dimensions of God's hopes for us? If we regularly take the lids off of our imagination, there may be room to receive the extraordinary love and vision of God in the foggy recesses of our daily lives. Are you, in some way, looking for a rainbow in a black and white world?

During childhood summers, hearty meals at my grandmothers' tables fed my body and heightened my senses. Turquoise blue glasses were filled with cold milk poured from glass bottles. Icy green 7-Up bottles lined the door of the "ice box." Grandmother's vines groaned with plump, fire-engine red tomatoes from which she peeled the slippery skin before showering them with salt and flakes of freshly-ground black pepper. We would pick corn from her garden where my grandfather had thoughtfully planted every other row with yellow corn and then sweet white corn, because he preferred one and she the other. And then just before dinner I would go around the side of the house to pick fresh mint for the iced tea. The bed was near the hose connection where occasional drips of water caused the mint to proliferate. The smell of mint rubbed on my fingers today brings these culinary memories tumbling back in vivid greens, blues, reds, and yellows. For my young, fussy palate, Grandmother's table was a rainbow of the finest foods born of Kansas soil. Such an earthly table was a precursor to my understanding of one holy table, set by God long ago in an upper room. Red wine, white unleavened bread, and the deepest color of Divine love transformed a black and white world.

From "Looking For a Rainbow," Patricia M.B. Kitchen

O God of prisms and kaleidoscopes, of azure seas and coral sunsets, forgive me when I walk through any day with a corrugated cardboard attitude. Throw open my mind to the holy possibilities you may be nudging me toward. When I stubbornly see only black and white solutions, pour your diverse palette upon my pessimism. Amen.

"The sun illuminates their kingdom"

*My child, do not let these escape from your sight: Keep sound
wisdom and prudence, and they will be life for your soul and
adornment for your neck. Then you will walk on your way
securely and your foot will not stumble. If you sit down, you
will not be afraid; when you lie down, your sleep will be
sweet. Do not be afraid of sudden panic, or of the storm that
strikes the wicked; for the Lord will be your confidence and
will keep your foot from being caught.*
Proverbs 3:21-26

Young Kings of Bermuda

The vast beaches and the sapphire water play home
to a young man's dream
He stands atop the smooth rock aside his counterpart;
they are kings
They yell at the top of their lungs because they are free;
and the fish swim below
They plunge into the blue and their subjects disperse;
the sun illuminates their kingdom
They tour their realm on their two-wheeled chariots
and visit the plush green land where
White spheres soar through the temperate air;
They continue on to Hamilton where the vast ships
have assembled. They coast along the shoreline,

riding like knights on their stallions.
Riding up the twisting road towards
their magnificent castle, it is there
that they are shown to their throne. Carried by
the ascending mechanical bird, they cross
the threshold into their own space, away
from the rest of the kingdom,
Where they sit and make colossal decisions
Like which kind of ice cream to eat next.

Crawford F. Brubaker III

How vividly I remember the simplicity of being a child. Let me never forget, O Lord, the whimsy and wonder that fills the soul of youth. Fill me with a spirit of gratitude for cool water, for crackling fireplaces, for hot morning coffee, and for icy orange juice. For having limbs to stretch and eyes to see far, I am grateful, God. Now I pray for my imagination to be reignited. I want to dive in cold water and take a wild risk once in a while. Life feels so serious some days; I pray to remember the whimsy of my youth . . . and to act upon my impulses a little more often. Amen.

"What are your personal pillars?"

Let the words of my mouth
And the meditation of my heart
Be acceptable in thy sight,
O Lord, my rock and my redeemer.
Psalm 19:14

The people who survived the sword
found grace in the wilderness;
when Israel sought for rest,
the Lord appeared to him from afar.
I have loved you with an everlasting love;
Therefore I have continued my faithfulness to you.
Jeremiah 31:2-3

WHAT ARE YOUR personal pillars? What framework structures your life, your choices, your checkbook? One element of Outward Bound which caught me by surprise was its philosophy, its four pillars. They are: 1) self-reliance 2) physical fitness 3) craftsmanship 4) service, or compassion, toward nature and others. I headed south in September expecting the first two components; frankly, concerned by how far they might push the physical fitness and self-reliance aspects. I assumed it would be a dirty, rugged weekend fit for Diana Nyad or Mia Hamm and not for me. But my crew was led by two superb young women who taught us to climb rocks, find our bearings with a compass, tie knots, rappel cliffs, and trust total strangers, without ever sacrificing craftsmanship or compassion.

Is God tugging at you to try something new? Where are we too comfortable? Let the world scratch its head as we take inventory and restock the shelves of our lives.

From "Inward Bound," Patricia M.B. Kitchen

What really matters in the course of a life, O God? The answer seems to change from one decade to another. So I pray for clear direction. But even more so, I pray for a deep sense of trust so that when I feel misdirected or my purposes are muddled, I will sense the compass of your Spirit leading my way. I pray for clarity of thought and a disciplined mind, that I might take the time to realign my priorities with your deepest longings. Amen.

"What we get from this adventure is just sheer joy"

But the fruit of the Spirit is love, joy, peace, patience, kindness, goodness, faithfulness, gentleness, self-control; against such there is no law.
Galatians 5:22-23

I lift up my eyes to the hills.
From whence does my help come?
My help comes from the Lord,
Who made heaven and earth.
He will not let your foot be moved,
He who keeps you will not slumber.
Behold, he who keeps Israel
Will neither slumber nor sleep.
Psalm 121:1-4

THE FIRST QUESTION which you will ask and which I must try to answer is this: "What is the use of climbing Mount Everest?" and my answer must be at once "It is no use." There is not the slightest prospect of gain whatsoever. Oh, we may learn a little about the behavior of the human body at high altitudes where there is only a third of an atmosphere, and possibly the doctors may turn our observation to some account for the purposes of aviation. But otherwise nothing will come of it. We shall not bring back a single bit of gold or silver, not a gem, not any coal or iron. We shall not find a foot of earth that can be planted with crops to raise food. It's no use.

So if you cannot understand that there is something in us which responds to the challenge of this mountain and goes out to meet it, that the struggle is the struggle of life itself upward and forever upward, then you won't see why we go.

What we get from this adventure is just sheer joy. And joy is, after all, the end of life. We do not live to eat and make money. We eat and make money to be able to enjoy life. That is what life means and what life is for.

George Leigh Mallory (1886–1924)

May the steps I take this day be ones directed toward adventure, O Lord. If not external physical adventure then internal voyages. For I worry a bit that I'm becoming physically and emotionally sedate. Grant me growth, I pray. And then enable me to experience the joy you intend for your creation! Amen.

"Life and death stared one another in the face"

Now there is in Jerusalem by the sheep gate a pool, in Hebrew called Bethzatha, which has five porticoes. In these lay a multitude of invalids, blind, lame, paralyzed. One man was there, who had been ill for thirty-eight years. When Jesus saw him and knew that he had been lying there a long time, he said to him, "Do you want to be healed?" The sick man answered him, "Sir, I have no man to put me into the pool when the water is troubled, and while I am going another steps down before me." Jesus said to him, "Rise, take up your pallet, and walk." And at once the man was healed, and he took up his pallet and walked.
John 5:1-9

ON A SEPTEMBER Saturday in 1970, Dr. James Loder, a professor at Princeton Theological Seminary, set forth traveling in a camper from Princeton, New Jersey to Quebec, Canada with his wife and two young daughters. It was an exceptional day, "lifted from a travel poster," he says. But by 4:30 that afternoon, the beauty of the day had been bathed in excruciating pain.

Heading north on the interstate, Dr. Loder saw a middle-aged woman beside her disabled Oldsmobile, waving a white glove for help, precariously near the roaring traffic. Alarmed and dutiful, the Loders pulled off the road to offer help to the two travelers. It was a simple flat tire. Unable to get the wobbly jack to lock into the chassis on the left front side, Dr. Loder moved to the right wheel looking for a helpful clue. Just as he knelt down in front of the fender, there was an ear-splitting screech of brakes. A 64-year-old man, with a perfect driving record, had fallen asleep at the wheel for an instant. The driver's car rammed the back of the Oldsmobile which proceeded to smash into the rear of the Loder's camper, pinning Dr. Loder under the car. The two traveling women were injured in the collision, which left only Mrs. Loder, a petite woman barely over five feet tall, to help. Arlene Loder put her hands under the pumper, prayed fervently, and lifted. In the intense effort of heaving, Mrs. Loder lost consciousness for a few seconds – and broke a vertebra – and when she refocused she was stunned to see that the car had been lifted, enabling Dr. Loder to breathe and be freed from the clutches of the car. Something holy had happened in that moment.

I am not one to be dazzled by fantastic tales of divine appearances or intervention. My logic too often gets in the way. But when I passed Dr. Loder walking across the Princeton campus, and heard him speak of "the transforming moment," that transpired that day, I became aware that something real had changed the course of his life. Dr. Loder said that all of his Harvard training and European post-doctoral work and honors, all of his rational, philosophical notions of theology melted on the hot pavement of the expressway – where one man encountered God, not in books or brains, but in an unexpected moment when life and death stared one another in the face.

Dare we trust that God will move within highly educated, heavily guarded hearts or within lives timed with precision, cooked to order, starched, and shelved?

From "Expecting the Unexpected," Patricia M.B. Kitchen

O Lord, help us to turn off the clocks that bind our time with Thee. As we shed the conventions which mar our openness to Thy Spirit, fill the shallow spaces of our lives with the depth of Thy love. Save us from the necessity of having to meet death to encounter Thee, but rather in our living, may our souls be transformed and our waking hours directed toward holy love and justice for all. Amen.

"Holy and unscheduled surprises"

The angel of the Lord appeared to Moses in a flame of fire out of the midst of a bush; and he looked, and lo, the bush was burning, yet it was not consumed. And Moses said, "I will turn aside and see this great sight, why the bush is not burnt." When the Lord saw that he turned aside to see, God called to him out of the bush, "Moses, Moses!" And he said, "Here am I."
Exodus 3:2-4

SOME 3,000 years ago, Moses took a closer look at an odd bush on a hillside of Mt. Horeb. Moses was shepherding the flock of his father-in-law Jethro. And there, in the middle of an ordinary afternoon, the Lord appeared to him in a flame of fire rising from a scruffy bush. Moses looked, and looked again, and the bush was blazing, yet it was not consumed. It was an extraordinary flame, an unexpected flame, fueled by the very mystery of God that stuns us all with holy and unscheduled surprises. And here lies the challenge: if we become consumed by our modern-day shepherding, whether it be clients, patients, stocks and bonds, parenting, shops, or schools, we may miss the burning bush where God attempts to catch our attention. Our powers of observation must be heightened lest we move through life in spiritual straitjackets.

Moses knew when to sit still and stare into the fire we call faith. If Moses had worn a Seiko watch or had a travel alarm clock ticking in his tent, he may have thrown a quizzical glance toward that mystifying bush but then quickly moved on to his shepherding duties.

Have you noticed when God attempts to slip into your life? Perhaps not boldly through a conventional front door labeled "Religion," but through an unexpected, unmarked side door to quietly affect the course of your life?

From "Expecting the Unexpected," Patricia M.B. Kitchen

Sometimes you show up in the most unexpected places, O God. Remind me, when I think I have a good grip on faith, that you are a God of surprises. Amen.

PART II

Daring to Dream

"Come wake me up"

Awake, O north wind, and come, O south wind!
Blow upon my garden, let its fragrance be wafted abroad.
Let my beloved come to his garden, and eat its choicest fruits.
Song of Solomon 4:16

How precious also are Thy thoughts to me, O God! How vast
is the sum of them! If I should count them, they would out-
number the sand. When I am awake, I am still with Thee.
Psalm 139:17-18

Then the word of the Lord came to me saying, "Son of
man, you live in the midst of the rebellious house, who
have eyes to see but do not see, ears to hear but do not hear;
for they are a rebellious house. Therefore, son of man, pre-
pare for yourself baggage for exile and go into exile by day
in their sight; even go into exile from your place to another
place in their sight. Perhaps they will understand though
they are a rebellious house."
Ezekiel 12:1-3

K EEP ME from going to sleep too soon. Or if I go to
sleep too soon, come wake me up. Come whistling up the
road. Stomp on the porch. Bang on the door. Make me get out
of bed and come and let you in and light a light. Tell me the
Northern Lights are on and make me look. Or tell me clouds

are doing something to the moon they never did before, and show me. See that I see. Talk to me 'til I'm half as wide awake as you and start to dress wondering why I ever went to bed at all. Tell me that waking is superb. Not only tell me but persuade me. You know I'm not too hard to persuade.

Robert Francis (1901–1987)

MORNING IS WHEN I am awake and there is a dawn in me. Moral reform is the effort to throw off sleep. Why is it that men give so poor an account of their day if they have not been slumbering? . . . The millions are awake enough for physical labor; but only one in a million is awake enough for effective intellectual exertion, only one in a hundred million to a poetic or divine life. To be awake is to be alive. . . . We must learn to reawaken and keep ourselves awake, not by mechanical aids, but by an infinite expectation of the dawn, which does not forsake us in our soundest sleep.

Henry David Thoreau (1817–1862)

Awaken me, I pray, to the world surrounding me, pulsating with everything from the morning honking of horns to the scratching legs of crickets at dusk. Awaken my senses to the thousand shades of green around me and to the cumulus clouds playing alongside the cirrus ones. Awaken my inner world even more so, I pray. Where my soul sleeps, let me hear the strains of a new symphony sounding a stirring chord progression, luring me out of any self-centeredness or complacency that threatens to numb my waking hours. I pray for an "infinite expectation of the dawn," and then to dress and go out into the world cloaked in love and justice. Amen.

12

"Creeping separateness"

*"Behold, I will do something new, now it will spring forth;
will you not be aware of it? I will even make a roadway in
the wilderness, rivers in the desert."*
Isaiah 43:19

I STUMBLED ACROSS a story in the August issue of *Town and
Country*. A story in which one family had to consciously
turn the tide against creeping separateness. Their way was to retreat to a sparse setting in order to reconnect. Often times I sense
we simply need to retreat right where we are. Slowing the pace,
enabling the Divine to connect with a deeper place in our souls.

In this particular article entitled "A Simple Summer Place,"
Charles Gaines got my attention in the first paragraph as he
described what we have called "creeping separateness" and how
it almost killed his marriage and his family. He tells the poi-
gnant tale of rebuilding these critical relationships in a one-
room cabin in Nova Scotia, fashioned by his own inexperi-
enced hands. He was a writer, not a carpenter. Gaines describes
how the 1980s "had been both easy and hard on us, as they
had been on a lot of people. We had acquired much of what
we had dreamed of having and worked to have, but we had
lost more . . . both of our fathers . . . a brother-in-law and a beloved
friend. A business I had no business starting had failed, as had
both my hip joints. . . . And, somewhere, Patricia and I had lost

the cohesive, protective intimacy of family life. . . . For a while there in the eighties, we even lost each other." Creeping separateness. After the children left, Gaines says their home was like a "beautiful but suddenly desolate town in which a war has just been fought; you and the town have survived, if barely, but the war has made you a stranger there for good." They turned to a simple, one-room cabin, and the sweat and groans of erecting it took "fresh effort and initiative . . . to craft a new life." The key is the fresh effort, not the cabin. We do not have to leave our cities or towns to craft a new life . . . but we may need to change, simplify, or rebuild something that is here.

From "Creeping Separateness," Patricia M.B. Kitchen

We long to be washed anew, O Lord. On days when we feel charred and exhausted, breathe hope into our weary bones, we pray. Wipe the cynical dust from our eyes, and help us to see new vistas before us. Cleanse us, renew us, and send us out into this day bathed in grace. Amen.

13

"The stars touch the road"

And God took Abraham outside and said, "Now look toward
the heavens, and count the stars, if you are able to count them."
And God said to him, "So shall your descendants be."
Genesis 15:5

JUST TRY COUNTING them, all of them . . ." God encouraged
Abraham. And then God turned to Abraham, who had
never held a child of his own, looked him in the eye and
said, "So shall your descendants be. Count them, Abraham,
and when your eyes feel sandy with sleep and you can count
no more, count a few more and then go into your tent and
sleep, believing in the creative extravagance of my love for
you and Sarah."

When I lived in Los Angeles it was often frustrating to sit
outside in the evening, to look up into the night sky, and see
only haze of the day's leftover smog and the gray blur of a
million city lights mixed with what should have been the
black of night. It was not possible to see stars, much less
count them or find the Big Dipper or Orion's belt. But two
summers ago I traveled to Ellsworth, Kansas, where the open
sky is uninterrupted by very little except the golden light of
fireflies . . . and after my grandmother's 104th birthday
dinner and a remarkable double rainbow that seemed to
crown her day, I asked my mother and father to drive me to

the edge of the little town because my cousin had told me of the feast of stars that blanket the Kansas skies from that vantage point. During the summers of my childhood, I had seen many evening skies from the little hill where my grandparents lived, but Susan said the stars touch the road when you move away from even the slim glow of street and porch lights.

And it was true.

And it was stunning.

I tell you about the Kansas stars because the one thought that has stuck with me since that unusual July night is that we bear the same faith Abraham did so long ago. God asks us to go forth into unfamiliar territory and it can be frightening sometimes. Yes, it is the same God pointing to the same stars, and the same God leading the way onto unventured plains of faith. Where do you need to go, with a bundle of faith upon your back?

From *"L'Amour de Dieu est Folie,"* Patricia M.B. Kitchen

We lift our eyes, O God, and long to see a glimpse of something greater than the drumbeat of daily demands. Grant us new perspective. Forgive us when we get tangled in the knotted threads of pressing needs. Enable us, we pray, to see beyond the temporary to that which is eternal. Amen.

14

"What happens to a dream deferred?"

"And it will come about after this
That I will pour out My Spirit on all mankind;
And your sons and daughters will prophesy,
Your old men will dream dreams,
Your young men will see visions."
Joel 2:28

Tell Me

Why should it be *my* loneliness,
Why should it be *my* song,
Why should it be *my* dream
        deferred
        overlong?

Harlem

What happens to a dream deferred?

        Does it dry up
        Like a raisin in the sun?
        Or fester like a sore –
        And then run?
        Does it stink like rotten meat?
        Or crust and suger over –
        Like a syrupy sweet?

Maybe it just sags
Like a heavy load.

Or does it explode?

Poems by Langston Hughes (1902–1967)

God, grant me the vision to be daring in my dreams; point
me toward problems that require bold insight and then enable me to articulate the possibilities. Amen.

15

"Live deep
and suck out all the marrow of life"

Keep your life free from love of money, and be content with what you have; for he has said, "I will never fail you nor forsake you."
Hebrews 13:5

Wash yourselves; make yourselves clean;
Remove the evil of your doings from before my eyes;
Cease to do evil, learn to do good;
Seek justice, correct oppression;
Defend the fatherless, plead for the widow.
Isaiah 1:16-17

I WENT TO THE WOODS because I wished to live deliberately, to front only the essential facts of life, and see if I could not learn what it had to teach, and not, when I came to die, discover that I had not lived. I did not wish to live what was not life, living is so dear; nor did I wish to practice resignation, unless it was quite necessary. I wanted to live deep and suck out all the marrow of life, to live so sturdily and Spartanlike as to put to rout all that was not life.

From *Walden* by Henry David Thoreau (1817–1862)

Sometimes I feel as though I function daily on automatic pilot. Jar me, I pray. Shake me gently, but firmly, lest I find myself slipping into a deep rut. Help me to uncover the essence of life. Open my eyes to unusual people, out-of-the-way places, new music, tastes, smells and passions. Just please do not let me fall asleep walking through life. Amen.

16

"Great changes"

Then spoke Joshua to the Lord in the day when the Lord gave the Amorites over to the men of Israel; and he said in the sight of Israel,

"Sun, stand thou still at Gibeon, and thou Moon in the valley of Ai'jalon."

And the sun stood still, and the moon stayed, until the nation took vengeance on their enemies.

Is this not written in the Book of Jashar? The sun stayed in the midst of heaven, and did not hasten to go down for about a whole day. There has been no day like it before or since, when the Lord hearkened to the voice of a man; for the Lord fought for Israel.

Joshua 10:12-14

Now as he journeyed he approached Damascus, and suddenly a light from heaven flashed about him. And he fell to the ground and heard a voice saying to him, "Saul, Saul, why do you persecute me?" And he said, "Who are you, Lord?" And he said, "I am Jesus, whom you are persecuting; but rise and enter the city, and you will be told what you are to do." The men who were traveling with him stood speechless, hearing the voice but seeing no one.

Acts 9:3-7

THAT WAS a memorable day to me, for it made great changes in me. But it is the same with any life. Imagine one selected day struck out of it, and think how different its course would have been. Pause, you who read this, and think for a moment of the long chain of iron or gold, of thorns or flowers, that would never have bound you, but for the formation of the first link on one memorable day.

From *Great Expectations* by Charles Dickens (1812–1870)

Looking back, I see the times where the light of a person's love or the strength of another's courage altered my life in an unusual way. O God, I pray that I will be so alert in the course of daily living that I can be light for another, be strong for one entrapped in pain, be optimistic for one lacking hope, be jubilant with one who celebrates. Help me to see the nuances of your vast love as they seep into the river of life. Amen.

17

"Let love be genuine, hate what is evil, hold fast to what is good"

My son, eat honey, for it is good,
and the drippings of the honeycomb are sweet to your taste.
Know that wisdom is such to your soul;
if you find it, there will be a future,
and your hope will not be cut off.
Proverbs 24:13-14

Let love be genuine; hate what is evil, hold fast to what is good;
love one another with brotherly affection; outdo one another in
showing honor. Never flag in zeal, be aglow with the Spirit,
serve the Lord. Rejoice in your hope, be patient in tribulation,
be constant in prayer. Contribute to the needs of the saints, prac-
tice hospitality. Bless those who persecute you; bless and do not
curse them. Rejoice with those who rejoice, weep with those who
weep. Live in harmony with one another; do not be haughty,
but associate with the lowly; never be conceited. Repay no one
evil for evil, but take thought for what is noble in the sight of all.
If possible, so far as it depends upon you, live peaceably with all.
Romans 12:9-18

THERE CAN BE no doubt that the young of today have to be protected against certain poisonous effects inherent in present-day civilization. Five social diseases surround them, even in early childhood. There is the decline in fitness, due to the modern methods of locomotion; the decline in initiative, due to the widespread disease of spectatoritis; the decline in care and skill, due to the weakened tradition of quality; the decline in self-discipline, due to the ever-present availability of tranquilizers and the stimulants; the decline of compassion, which William Temple called "spiritual death."

Kurt Hahn, founder of Outward Bound (edited)

God of strength and of compassion, of excellence and endurance, quicken my mind and my spirit, I pray. Where sloth seeps in and lulls me into complacency, jar me from apathy, I pray. Where peers or colleagues jeer and lure me toward unhealthy or destructive activity, strengthen my spine, I pray. Light fireworks of new energy and initiative within me that I might seek excellence, strive toward a higher good, and not settle for substandard principles, thoughts or actions. Amen.

18

"The hourglass whispers
to the lion's roar"

Sow for yourselves righteousness,
Reap the fruit of steadfast love;
Break up your fallow ground,
For it is the time to seek the Lord,
That he may come and rain salvation upon you.
Hosea 10:12

Our Bias

The hour-glass whispers to the lion's roar,
The clock-towers tell the gardens day and night,
How many errors Time has patience for,
How wrong they are in being always right.

Yet time, however loud its chimes or deep,
However fast its falling torrent flows,
Has never put one lion off his leap
Nor shaken the assurance of a rose.

For they, it seems, care only for success:
While we choose words according to their sound
And judge a problem by its awkwardness;

And time with us was always popular.

When have we not preferred some going round
To going straight to where we are?
W.H. Auden (1907–1973)

Dear Lord, when time races, I stumble. When it stands still, I am impatient. When time holds me hostage, I cry for freedom. When it hums a sane tune, I rejoice. Grant me a light hand upon my watch and a restful eye upon the clock. Remind me, when I most need to be so, that all time rests securely in your holy will. Amen.

PART III

Simplicity and Sabbath

19

"Clutter . . . what are we doing with so much of it anyway?"

"Do not lay up for yourselves treasures upon earth, where moth and rust destroy, and where thieves break in and steal. But lay up for yourselves treasures in heaven, where neither moth nor rust destroys, and where thieves do not break in or steal; for where your treasure is, there will your heart be also."
Matthew 6:19-21

Behold, you are beautiful, my beloved, truly lovely. Our couch is green; the beams of our house are cedar, our rafters are pine.
Song of Solomon 1:16-17

HONESTLY, if it had not been for this North Carolina Outward Bound experience I would have focused this sermon on love or eschatology or the Parable of the Talents. But I am mentally stuck back at base camp in the Pisgah National Forest of North Carolina, where we pared our belongings down to a thread prior to our four-day trek. The sun setting over the layers of blue ridges became our cinema. And cool water was our evening aperatif. Our first task was to carefully fill our backpacks with only fifty pounds of necessities . . . which included packing, in essence, the kitchen sink, stove, and a bedroom upon our backs. So there was no room left for flannel nightgowns and slippers or even a good book. Before setting off along those dusty, rocky, mountain trails we were eliminating excessive, superfluous, material possessions. . . . Things, stuff, clutter. . . . What are we doing with so much of it anyway?

From "Inward Bound," Patricia M.B. Kitchen

There is much, O God, that seems to weigh us down: bills and belongings, homework, repairs and appointments, responsibility and excess in many arenas of our lives. Help us to pare down, we pray. Enable us to see the line between needing and wanting. Grant us the holiness of simplicity in daily life. Amen.

20

"It may be time to take inventory of our lives"

"For this reason I say to you, do not be anxious for your life, as to what you shall eat, or what you shall drink; nor for your body, as to what you shall put on. Is not life more than food, and the body than clothing? Look at the birds of the air, that they do not sow, neither do they reap, nor gather into barns, and yet your heavenly Father feeds them. Are you not worth much more than they? And which of you by being anxious can add a single cubit to his life's span? And why are you anxious about clothing? Observe how the lilies of the field grow; they do not toil nor do they spin, yet I say to you that even Solomon in all his glory did not clothe himself like one of these. But if God so arrays the grass of the field, which is alive today and tomorrow is thrown into the furnace, will He not much more do so for you, O men of little faith?"
Matthew 6:25-30

CONSIDER THE LILIES and regain perspective. I wonder how often we think, "If I just had _____ ." Fill in the blank. Then consider the lilies. We can pray for fresh perspective. We can get honest about the difference between wanting and needing and try to help our children redefine those terms. Think about it. Where do you spend your time? Where do you spend your money? What fills your closets and cupboards and drawers? What fills your heart? What ideas fill your mind and conversations? It may be time to take inventory of our lives.

From "Inward Bound," Patricia M.B. Kitchen

Lord, there seems to be something seductive about complexity. A chorus of alluring advertisements dangle temptations before us. We scoop things up and then cannot find the time to use them or the space to store them. But we cannot quite imagine life scaled back. Encourage us to find our sense of self within your Divine Presence and not in the reflection of possessions. Amen.

21

"Inner chaos can be realigned by grace"

Better is a dry morsel with quiet, than a house full of feasting with strife.
Proverbs 17:1

Do not be conformed to this world but be transformed by the renewal of our mind, that you may prove what is the will of God, what is good and acceptable and perfect.
Romans 12:2

ON THE ELEVENTH of the fourteen Tuesday visits, Morrie and Mitch talked more about our culture. Morrie explained, "Here's what I mean by building your own little subculture. . . . I don't mean you disregard every rule of your community. I don't go around naked, for example. I don't run through red lights. The little things, I can obey. But the big things - how you think, what we value - those you must choose yourself. You can't let anyone - or any society - determine those for you. . . . Every society has its own problems. . . . The way to do it, I think, isn't to run away."

The predominant culture seems to be one of working, meeting, spending, and consuming. While we must dwell in the practical sphere of productivity required of us, daily reality can be reshaped by Divine love. Inner chaos can be realigned by grace.

From "Sundays With Morrie," Patricia M.B. Kitchen;

based on the book *Tuesdays With Morrie* by Mitch Albom

In the quiet of these few minutes, still my soul, I pray. Where appointments and clients and meals and voices clamor for urgent attention, help me to step back far enough from the race of each day to regain perspective. Help me to build a sub-culture of sorts where patience and peace prevail. Let me not succumb to any unhealthy drive within me or around me. Center me, I pray, surrounded by your calm, steady Presence. Amen.

22

"The power of the world always works in circles"

For everything there is a season,
*   and a time for every matter under heaven:*
A time to be born, and a time to die;
A time to plant, and a time to pluck up what is planted;
A time to kill, and a time to heal;
A time to break down, and a time to build up;
A time to weep, and a time to laugh;
A time to mourn, and a time to dance;
A time to cast away stones,
*   and a time to gather stones together;*
A time to embrace, and a time to refrain from embracing;
A time to seek, and a time to lose;
A time to keep, and a time to cast away;
A time to rend, and a time to sew;
A time to keep silence, and a time to speak;
A time to love, and a time to hate;
A time for war, and a time for peace.
Ecclesiastes 3:1-8

YOU HAVE NOTICED that everything that an Indian does is in a circle and that is because the power of the world always works in circles and everything tries to be round. In the old days when we were a strong and happy people, all our power came to us from the sacred loop of the nation and so long as the loop was unbroken, the people flourished. The flowering tree was the living center of the loop and the circle of the four quarters nourished it. The east gave peace and light, the south gave warmth, the west gave rain, and the north with its cold and mighty wind gave strength and endurance. Everything the power of the world does is done in a circle. The sky is round and I have heard that the earth is round like a ball and so are all the stars. The wind, in its greatest power, whirls. Birds make their nests in a circle. The sun comes forth and goes down again in a circle. . . . Even the seasons form a great circle in their changing and always coming back again to where they were. The life of a person is a circle from childhood to childhood and so it is in everything where power is.

From *Black Elk Speaks* by Black Elk and John Neihardt, 1932

When time whirrs with good times and laughter and loud, joyous music, I'm grateful, O God. When time screams with pain and misunderstanding, I'm confused, O God. When time moves slowly and lulls me into a place of peace, I'm glad to be still, O God. Enable me to wait when I am out of step with the rhythm of a healthy life. When time will not keep pace with my desires, awaken me to your holy will. Amen.

23

"Head for the hills and pray"

The apostles gathered around Jesus and told him all that they had done and taught. He said to them, "Come away to a deserted place all by yourselves and rest a while." For many were coming and going, and they had no leisure even to eat. And they went away in the boat to a deserted place by themselves.

Mark 6:30-32

WHEN WE SKIM the fifth and sixth chapters of Mark's Gospel, we see one miracle after another performed. Jesus was busy. He had already incorporated the principle of management through delegation by calling twelve disciples to work alongside him. But even with their help, Jesus was busy. He addressed crowds daily, taught brilliant parables, calmed the sea that week, and healed the Gerasene man full of demons, Jairus's twelve-year-old dying daughter, and the woman who had been hemorrhaging for twelve years. Jesus was busy. And so were the disciples. There was so much healing that needed to happen that Jesus dispersed the disciples and sent them out in teams of two. Everybody was working overtime and torn apart by the news that Jesus' cousin, John the Baptist, had been beheaded by Herod. So finally one day, the disciples returned "and gathered around Jesus, and told him all they had done and taught." They were exhausted. Stress existed in the first century. So Jesus said to them, "Come away, to a deserted place all by yourselves and rest awhile." Camp David for the disciples. "For many were coming and going and they had no leisure even to eat." No Wendy's to drive through for a grilled chicken sandwich and a frosty. No microwaves on their mission trips. The disciples were exhausted and hungry. And Jesus was almost always busy. But he knew when to stop and get in a boat and head for the other side of the lake, or head for the hills and pray. Jesus demonstrated for us the rhythm of physical work and spiritual rest. There was a *healthy rhythm* to Jesus' life on earth. A rhythm prompted by the internal question, "What is truly *important* versus what is only *urgent?*" Jesus set a holy rhythm of responsibility and rest. And he knew when to slow down and ask what was important, rather than be swept up in a frenzy of urgency. Sometimes he knew that meant getting to the other side of the lake to be still and to pray.

What is "the other side of the lake" for you? Where or how do you allow room for the holy rhythm of responsibility and rest?
From "Walking on Water After Dinner," Patricia M.B. Kitchen

Grant us peace in the maze of daily living, O Lord; give us the willpower to step back from the frenzy of an overly active existence and to seek calm in the midst of the gusts of commitments. Help us to find a healthy rhythm of both responsibility and rest and to hear your still, calm voice in both. Amen.

24

"Contemplating what to do or where to go?"

Teach me, and I will be silent;
And show me how I have erred.
Job 6:24

For God alone my soul waits in silence . . .
Psalm 62:1

Be angry, but sin not;
Commune with your own hearts
On your beds, and be silent.
Psalm 4:4

Be still, and know that I am God.
Psalm 46:10

A Reflection Upon Painted Water

Contemplating what to do or where to go?
No, the currents move, the tides go in and out,
      but he remains the same.
He sits back and watches as love, laughter, faith
      and friendship pass him by
Drifting through life, he needs no direction
He is calm like the water surrounding his tiny boat
When the wind blows, he follows, destination unknown
A tempest arises but he does not falter

Drifting through life, he needs no direction

He leaves no wake for others to observe
            but moves contentedly along
The oars lay lifelessly in the water,
            waiting for initiative to take over
They are forgotten and begin to rot
Drifting through life, letting time slip away

Men like him come and go just like the tides
They are men who build sand castles
And their castles are washed away
            just as quickly as they were built
Drifting through life, letting time slip away
Crawford F. Brubaker III

TO PRESERVE the silence within – amid all the noise. To remain open and quiet, a moist humus in the fertile darkness where the rain falls and the grain ripens – no matter how many tramp across the parade ground in whirling dust under an arid sky.
Dag Hammerskjold (1905–1961)

Lord, I pray for new conviction. It really is easier to float along and not be concerned about poverty just a mile away, or the squandering of land for profit rather than for health and natural beauty. When I think about the children killed by irresponsible adults wielding guns or driving drunk, my insides knot. But then I wonder if it is too hard to change myself or my world. Fill me with your Spirit, I pray. Fill me with purpose and direction. Fill me with fresh hope this day. Amen.

"There shall be a Sabbath"

The Lord spoke to Moses on Mount Sinai, saying: Speak to the people of Israel and say to them: When you enter the land that I am giving you, the land shall observe a sabbath for the Lord. Six years you shall sow your field, and six years you shall prune your vineyard, and gather in their yield; but in the seventh year there shall be a sabbath of complete rest for the land, a sabbath for the Lord: you shall not sow your field or prune your vineyard. You shall not reap the aftergrowth of your harvest or gather the grapes of your unpruned vine: it shall be a year of complete rest for the land.

Leviticus 25:1-5

GO MY STUDENTS burn your books; buy yourselves stout shoes. Get away to the mountains, the deserts and the deepest recesses of the earth. In this way and no other will you gain a true knowledge of things and of their properties.

Peter Severinus, 1571

It must be true that wisdom rises in periods of rest, silence, and solitude. Not a knowledge that produces high scores, passes exams or picks rising stocks, but rather a way of clear thinking, framed in compassion. Grant me a spirit of self-discipline that knows when to stop, step back or stay home. Clear my head of any clamor that keeps me from focusing upon your holy ways. Instill in me a daily sense of Sabbath, I pray. Amen.

"Zebras, giraffes, and a Bermuda blue sea"

What gain has the worker from his toil? I have seen the business that God has given to the sons of men to be busy with. He has made everything beautiful in its time; also he has put eternity into man's mind, yet so that he cannot find out what God has done from the beginning to the end. I know that there is nothing better for them than to be happy and enjoy themselves as long as they live.
Ecclesiastes 3:9-12

Truly, I say to you, unless you turn and become like children, you will never enter the kingdom of heaven. Whoever humbles himself like this child, he is the greatest in the kingdom of heaven.
Matthew 18:3-4

During the darkest of days, when my faith was almost nil, I never quite turned completely away from our creative and genius God. I think, in part, a thin, yet durable thread of belief was spun from a few uncanny realities of nature. One is the existence of rainbows. Other such odd elements of nature are the existence of zebras and giraffes, and the states of Hawaii and Alaska. What is it that you notice in the natural world that causes you to scratch your head knowing there was a true Artist at work in the beginning of all time? Perhaps it is the migration of Canadian geese? Or the microscopic structure of a dragonfly wing? *It is a colorful God we worship.* It is not a black and white, neatly packaged, clear-cut, judgmental, prescriptive relationship God offers us. No. It is a relationship as rich and varied as the shades of blue in a Bermuda sea. It is a relationship inherently as vivid as the green in a Maine forest. *It is a colorful God we worship.* This is something adults can learn from children. God's vast love is as colorful as the flags outside the United Nations Building in New York City. It is as colorful as the skin, eyes, and hair of God's people in Nairobi, Nepal, China, Sweden, and the United States. *Who or what has provided color in your life when it felt dark?* A whimsical child? A mountain range? A tender grandparent? A raging river? Perhaps God?

Patricia M.B. Kitchen

Grant to me, O God, for this day, the unbridled joy of a child . . . the curiosity . . . the wonder . . . the simplicity of untarnished experience in the natural world. Why do I worry so about food, shelter and clothing? Help me to concentrate on those who lack fresh food, a dependable roof, or a warm jacket in winter. Let the energy-sapping details of daily life fall into proper perspective. I simply want to relish the background sounds of insects and birds in flight. I pray to let that which drains my spirit fall away and create room in my soul for a deep sense of justice toward humankind and toward the world we inhabit. Amen.

PART IV

Rugged Love

27

"Love bade me welcome, but my soul drew back"

I will heal their disloyalty; I will love them freely, for my anger has turned from them. I will be like the dew to Israel; he shall blossom like the lily; he shall strike root like the forests of Lebanon. His shoots shall spread out; his beauty shall be like the olive tree, and his fragrance like that of Lebanon. They shall again live beneath my shadow; they shall flourish as a garden; they shall blossom like the vine, their fragrance shall be like the wine of Lebanon.

Hosea 14:4-7

Love

> Love bade me welcome; yet my soul drew back,
> Guilty of dust and sin.
> But quick-eyed Love, observing me grow slack
> From my first entrance in,
> Drew nearer to me, sweetly questioning,
> If I lacked anything.
>
> "A guest," I answered, "worthy to be here."
> Love said, "You shall be he."
> "I, the unkind, ungrateful? Ah, my dear,
> I cannot look on thee."
> Love took my hand, and smiling did reply,
> "Who made the eyes but I?"

"Truth, Lord, but I have marred them; let my shame
Go where it doth deserve."
"And know you not," says Love, "who bore the blame?"
"My dear, then I will serve."
"You must sit down," says Love, "and taste my meat."
So I did sit and eat.

George Herbert (1593–1633)

Sometimes it is hard to picture your love, O God. But I see it when justice prevails; I feel it in long-lasting relationships; I sense it in sacrificial giving; I hear it in passionate words spoken or sung. But it is hard to comprehend the breadth of Divine love. So I pray to glimpse one corner of it and then to pass it along where love is strained or absent. Amen.

28

"God's unconditional and irrational love"

No, in all these things we are more than conquerors through him who loved us. For I am sure that neither death, nor life, nor angels, nor principalities, nor things present, nor things to come, nor powers, nor height, nor depth, nor anything else in all creation, will be able to separate us from the love of God.

Romans 8:37-39

He brought me to the banqueting house, and his banner over me was love. Sustain me with raisins, refresh me with apples; for I am sick with love.

Song of Solomon 2:4-5

PERHAPS IT IS TRUE that God's love is incomprehensible to us and that language often deludes us when we attempt to explain such a love. God's actions, like God's love, are often irrational. And so the French Easter liturgy reads *"L' amour de Dieu est Folie"*: the love of God is foolishness. The French have captured the essence of God's unconditional and irrational love for our human folly. I spoke with a woman earlier this week who speaks a fair amount of French, and when I read the sermon title to her, she translated it as "The love of God . . . is crazy!" Her translation caught me off guard, but I thought about it and thought – yes, yes, that is true.

From "*L' Amour de Dieu est Folie,*" Patricia M.B. Kitchen

I have done nothing to warrant the depth of your love, and I know that. So I pray that I will live in such a way that I may pass along to another the transforming gift that comes from your Spirit. May sentences of affirmation spill from my lips; may I see strangers and those in great need through holy eyes rather than human rationale; may I be willing to sacrifice that to which I too often feel entitled, and instead, be generous in action and speech and faithful in prayer. Amen.

29

"The invincible summer"

The people who walked in darkness have seen a great light; Those who dwelt in a land of deep darkness, on them has light shined.
Isaiah 9:2

For lo, the winter is past,
The rain is over and gone.
The flowers appear on the earth,
The time of singing has come,
And the voice of the turtledove is heard in our land.
Song of Solomon 2:11-12

IN THE MIDST of winter
I finally learned
That there was in me
An invincible summer.
From "Return to Tipasa" by Albert Camus (1913–1960)

On His Blindness

When I consider how my light is spent,
Ere half my days, in this dark world and wide,
And that one talent which is death to hide
Lodged with me useless, though my soul more bent
To serve therewith my Maker, and present
My true account, lest he returning chide,
"Doth God exact day-labour, light denied?"

I fondly ask. But Patience, to prevent
That murmur, soon replies: "God doth not need
Either man's work or his own gifts; who best
Bear his mild yoke, they serve him best. His state
Is kingly: thousands at his bidding speed,
And post o'er land and ocean without rest;
They also serve who only stand and wait."
John Milton (1608–1674)

When the days feel frigid, whether it be the weather of my heart or the wind howling outdoors, melt my spirit, I pray. Let tenderness seep in where stubbornness prevails. May hope build a house within my heart that rests upon the foundation of your great mercy. Upon your promise to never leave or forsake us, I stand and see a horizon of hope that extends back to the tents and travels of Abraham and forward into eternity. Amen.

30

"Love bears all things,
believes all things,
hopes all things"

If I speak in the tongues of men and of angels, but have not love, I am a noisy gong or a clanging cymbal. And if I have prophetic powers, and understand all mysteries and all knowledge, and if I have all faith, so as to remove mountains, but have not love, I am nothing. If I give away all I have, and if I deliver my body to be burned, but have not love, I gain nothing.

Love is patient and kind; love is not jealous or boastful; it is not arrogant or rude. Love does not insist on its own way; it is not irritable or resentful; it does not rejoice at wrong, but rejoices in the right. Love bears all things, believes all things, hopes all things, endures all things.

Love never ends; as for prophecy, it will pass away; as for tongues, they will cease; as for knowledge, it will pass away. For our knowledge is imperfect and our prophecy is imperfect; but when the perfect comes, the imperfect will pass away. When I was a child, I spoke like a child, I thought like a child, I reasoned like a child; when I became a man, I gave up childish ways. For now we see in a mirror dimly, but then face to face. Now I know in part; then I shall understand fully, even as I have been fully understood. So faith, hope, love abide, these three; but the greatest of these is love.

I Corinthians 13

THE WORLD is not ruined by the wickedness of the wicked, but by the weakness of the good.

Napoleon (1769–1821)

Lord, make me an instrument of your peace.
Where there is hatred, let me sow love,
Where there is division, unity,
Where there is error, truth,
Where there is injury, pardon,
Where there is doubt, faith,
Where there is despair, hope,
Where there is darkness, light,
Where there is sadness, joy.
O Divine Master,
Grant that I may not so much seek
            to be consoled as to console,
To be understood as to understand,
To be loved as to love.
For it is in giving that we receive,
It is in pardoning that we are pardoned,
It is in dying that we are born to eternal life. Amen.

St. Francis of Assisi (1181–1226)

31

"The foremost task of education"

Blessed are the poor in spirit,
*   for theirs is the kingdom of heaven.*
Blessed are those who mourn,
*   for they shall be comforted.*
Blessed are the meek,
*   for they shall inherit the earth.*
Blessed are those who hunger and thirst for righteousness,
*   for they shall be satisfied.*
Blessed are the merciful,
*   for they shall obtain mercy.*
Blessed are the pure in heart,
*   for they shall see God.*
Blessed are the peacemakers,
*   for they shall be called sons of God.*
Blessed are those who are persecuted
*   for righteousness' sake,*
*   for theirs is the kingdom of heaven.*

Matthew 5:2-10

I REGARD IT as the foremost task of education to insure the survival of these qualities: an enterprising curiosity, an undefeatable spirit, tenacity in pursuit, readiness for sensible self-denial, and above all, compassion.

Kurt Hahn

May I move through this day
with a spirit of compassion,
with keen curiosity,
with an attitude of humility,
and an expansive vision of world peace.
May I move through this day
ready to serve one who hurts
even if it is unpleasant or inconvenient,
ready to ask hard or unusual questions
even if they are unpopular or outrageous,
ready to set aside my pride
even when I am tempted to boast,
and ready to act to bring peaceful resolve,
even when flames of anger or injustice
burn around or within me.
Lord, forgive my self-absorption and flood my soul
with your life-giving Spirit. Amen.

32

"The night is dark,
and I am far from home"

Not to us, O Lord, not to us, but to your name give glory,
For the sake of your steadfast love and your faithfulness.
Why should the nations say, "Where is their God?"
Our God is in the heavens;
He does whatever he pleases.
Their idols are silver and gold,
The work of human hands.
They have mouths, but do not speak;
Eyes, but do not see.
They have ears, but do not hear;
Noses, but do not smell.
They have hands, but do not feel;
Feet, but do not walk;
They make no sound in their throats.
Those who make them are like them;
So are all who trust in them.
O Israel, trust in the Lord!

Psalm 115:1-9

Lead, Kindly Light

> Lead, kindly Light, amid the encircling gloom,
>> Lead Thou me on;

The night is dark, and I am far from home,
    Lead Thou me on.
Keep Thou my feet; I do not ask to see
The distant scene; one step enough for me.

I was not ever thus, nor prayed that
    Thou shouldst lead me on;
I loved to choose and see my path;
    but now Lead Thou me on.
I loved the garish day, and, spite of fears,
Pride ruled my will: remember not past years.

So long Thy power hath blest me,
    sure it still will lead me on,
O'er moor and fen, o'er crag and torrent,
    till the night is gone;
And with the morn those Angel faces smile,
Which I have loved long since, and lost awhile.

John Henry Newman (1801–1890)

Some days it is too dark to trust, O Lord. All bulbs seem burned out. All candlelight extinguished. But old words waft across the marble counter of my memory bank . . . and my soul stirs just enough to turn and hear. Is it really true that You are the same yesterday, today, and forever? And that your love spans continents and more than one millennium? Then grant me to be still for long enough to hear old words once more and light the world anew. Amen.

33

"The prospect of forgiveness"

Though your sins are like scarlet, they shall be like snow;
though they are red like crimson, they shall become like wool.
Isaiah 1:18

Pray then in this way: Our Father in heaven, hallowed be
your name. Your kingdom come. Your will be done, on earth
as it is in heaven. Give us this day our daily bread. And forgive
us our debts, as we also have forgiven our debtors. And do not
bring us to the time of trial, but rescue us from the evil one. For
if you forgive others their trespasses, your heavenly Father will
also forgive you; but if you do not forgive others, neither will
your Father forgive your trespasses.
Matthew 6:9-15

I T IS TRUE, Father, that sometimes Heaven seems so far away;
and You know the hours when I am unsure of Your holy
will. Is it I who have wandered some distance? I wonder what
the aunts and mothers are thinking, whose children cry out
with stomach pain in Bangladesh, when they reach the words
"daily bread" in the prayer? But the most humbling phrase is
that of asking for the forgiveness of personal debts. Sometimes
the debts mount and I want to run from you, not toward your
merciful face. And, would you, I pray, show me *how* to ad-
equately forgive my debtors? Would you?

Patricia M.B. Kitchen

Dear God, when days seem long and I feel like I am drowning, then I turn to you. Help me to turn to you on dry land as well. I know I cannot repair my problems alone. Sometimes the prospect of forgiveness feels so remote. When the winds of grief roar and the storms of sorrow beat heedlessly, I try harder and harder to bail myself out. I pray for the strength to believe in your strength. I come running, stumbling, weeping rain which blurs my vision. Help me, I pray, to see you somehow in the midst of a pelting storm. Grant me the confidence that if I fully rely on you, the storms will calm, in time. I long to trust that when I fall at your feet, wet with old tears, you can put your finger to your lips and silence the rains saturating my soul. How does one move on through a storm? How does one forgive the hail caused by another? Amen.

34

"God irons out the wrinkles in our souls"

It shall be said, "Build up, build up, prepare the way, re-move every obstruction from my people's way." For thus says the high and lofty one who inhabits eternity, whose name is Holy: I dwell in the high and holy place, and also with those who are contrite and humble in spirit, to revive the spirit of the humble, and to revive the heart of the contrite.
Isaiah 57:14-15

Discipline

Throw away the rod,
Throw away thy wrath:
      O my God,
Take the gentle path.

For my heart's desire
Unto thine is bent:
      I aspire
To a full consent.

Not a word or look
I affect to own,
      But by book,
And thy book alone.

Though I fail, I weep:
Though I halt, I pace,

                    Yet I creep
To the throne of grace.

Then let wrath remove;
Love will do the deed
                    For with love
Stony hearts will bleed.

Love is swift of foot;
Love's a man of war,
                    And can shoot,
And can hit from far.

George Herbert (1593–1633)

Iron out the wrinkles in my soul, this hour, I pray. When life
feels a bit sloppy and in disarray, help me to see the difference between wrinkles in my exterior belongings and wrinkles
in my interior being. Grant me a sheet of grace on this day,
to pull up around my chin and help me to rest easy, upon
the bed of your Divine care. Amen.

35

"God moves in a mysterious way"

For the Lord your God is God of gods and Lord of lords, the great God, mighty and awesome, who is not partial and takes no bribe, who executes justice for the orphan and the widow, and who loves the strangers, providing them food and clothing. You shall also love the stranger, for you were strangers in the land of Egypt. You shall fear the Lord your God; him alone you shall worship; to him you shall hold fast, and by his name you shall swear. He is your praise; he is your God, who has done for you these great and awesome things that your own eyes have seen. Your ancestors went down to Egypt seventy persons; and now the Lord your God has made you as numerous as the stars in heaven.

Deuteronomy 10:17-22

Light Shining Out of Darkness

God moves in a mysterious way,
　　　　His wonders to perform;
He plants his footsteps in the sea,
　　　　And rides upon the storm.

Deep in unfathomable mines,
　　　　Of never failing skill
He treasures up his bright designs,
　　　　And works his sovereign will.

Ye fearful saints, fresh courage take,
        The clouds ye so much dread
Are big with mercy, and shall break,
        in blessings on your head.

Judge not the Lord by feeble sense,
        but trust him for his grace;
Behind a frowning providence,
        He hides a smiling face.

His purposes will ripen fast,
        Unfolding every hour;
The bud may have a bitter taste,
        But sweet will be the flower.

Blind unbelief is sure to err,
        And scan his work in vain;
God is his own interpreter,
        And he will make it plain.

William Cowper (1731–1800)

There are days, O Lord, when I feel bathed in the light of morning sun streaming across the lawn of my life. The loyalty of family, the humor of friends, the health of strong legs, and a tenderness of heart create a net of goodness. There were days I never thought the darkness would recede. Don't let me forget those lest I take for granted the light of this day. Will you, I pray, awaken me to dark corners in my world where the wattage of love or sacrificial service is now most needed? And then, urge me on unafraid of the dark, holding tightly to the candlestick of your holy light. Amen.

36

"She is in her grave, and oh, the difference to me!"

The Spirit of the Lord God is upon me, because the Lord has anointed me; he has sent me to bring good news to the oppressed, to bind up the brokenhearted, to proclaim liberty to the captives, and release to the prisoners; to proclaim the year of the Lord's favor, and the day of vengeance of our God; to comfort all who mourn; to provide for those who mourn in Zion – to give them a garland instead of ashes, the oil of gladness instead of mourning, the mantle of praise instead of a faint spirit.
Isaiah 61:1-3

She Dwelt Among the Untrodden Ways

She dwelt among the untrodden ways
    Beside the springs of Dove.
A Maid whom there were none to praise
    And very few to love;

A violet by a mossy stone
    Half hidden from the eye!
Fair as a star, when only one
    Is shining in the sky.

She lived unknown, and few could know
    When Lucy* ceased to be;

But she is in her grave, and, oh,
  The difference to me!

William Wordsworth (1770–1850)

*The poet's daughter, Catherine, who died at the age of four in 1812.

I believe, O God, that you dwell in some place or realm that is beyond human comprehension. I read once about a wrinkle in time that seems to describe in fantasy the intricacies of your eternal world. Grant me the peace to rest in the hammock of faith, knowing that your love defines the boundaries of eternal life. Amen.

37

"Death be not proud"

Listen, I will tell you a mystery! We will not all die, but we will all be changed, in a moment, in the twinkling of an eye, at the last trumpet. . . . When this perishable body puts on imperishablility, and this mortal body puts on immortality then the saying that is written will be fulfilled: "Death has been swallowed up in victory. Where, O death, is your victory? Where, O death, is your sting?"

I Corinthians 15:54-55

Death, Be Not Proud, Though Some Have Called Thee

Death, be not proud, though some have called thee
Mighty and dreadful, for thou art not so;
For those whom thou think'st thou dost overthrow
Die not, poor Death, nor yet canst thou kill me.
From rest and sleep, which but thy pictures be,
Much pleasure – then, from thee much more must flow;
And soonest our best men with thee do go,
Rest of their bones and soul's delivery.
Thou'rt slave to fate, chance, kings and desperate men,
And dost with poison, war, and sickness dwell;
And poppy or charms can make us sleep as well,
And better than thy stroke. Why swell'st thou then?
One short sleep past, we wake eternally,
And death shall be no more. Death, thou shalt die.

John Donne (1572–1631)

When the dusk of old age or persistent disease has veiled my vision and left me weary, grant me the hope of a lantern, lit down the road, protected from the wind, ready to welcome a spent body into the eternal presence of a God whose loving is unfathomable. There, I kneel and fall into the cocoon of your eternal care. Thanks be to God. Amen.

38

"To be a window, through thy grace"

O God, when you went out before your people,
when you marched through the wilderness,
The earth quaked, the heavens poured down rain
at the presence of God, the God of Sinai,
At the presence of God, the God of Israel.
Rain in abundance, O God, you showered abroad;
you restored your heritage when it languished;
Your flock found a dwelling in it; in your goodness,
O God, you provided for the needy.

Psalm 68:7-10

The Windows

Lord, how can man preach thy eternal word?
He is a brittle crazy glass;
Yet in thy temple thou dost him afford
This glorious and transcendent place,
To be a window, through thy grace.

But when thou dost anneal in glass thy story,
Making thy life to shine within
The holy preachers, then the light and glory
More reverend grows, and more doth win;
Which else shows waterish, bleak, and thin.

Doctrine and life, colors and light, in one

When they combine and mingle, bring
A strong regard and awe; but speech alone
Doth vanish like flaring thing,
And in the ear, not conscience, ring.

George Herbert (1593–1633)

Dear God, I give thanks for the brief moments when my soul surges with the electricity of new-found faith. Forgive my short span of hope. Show me the breadth of your will that I may settle down and be rooted in your holy way. Amen.

PART V

On Belay

"Human and divine connections"

The king was deeply moved, and went up to the chamber over the gate, and wept; and as he went, he said, "O my son Absalom, my son, my son Absalom! Would I had died instead of you, O Absalom, my son, my son!" It was told Joab, "The king is weeping and mourning for Absalom." So the victory that day was turned into mourning for all the troops; for the troops heard that day, "The king is grieving for his son."

II Samuel 18:33–19:2

Then Jonathan said to David, "Go in peace, since both of us have sworn in the name of the Lord, saying, 'The Lord shall be between me and you, and between my descendants and your descendants, forever.' "

I Samuel 20:42

Some friends play at friendship, but a true friend sticks closer than one's nearest kin.

Proverbs 18:24

ONE SEPTEMBER day in 1999, I stood on the precipice of a small cliff prepared to take my first step backward to rappel down the side of "Devil's Cellar." It was part of a North Carolina Outward Bound course, set in the Blue Ridge Mountains of Asheville, North Carolina. I suddenly froze in place as a fog of fear moved in on that sun-soaked mountainside. I stared into the blue eyes of my instructor as she calmly explained to me how very safe I was and why.

Then for one long minute, we remained motionless, in complete silence, as I debated internally the pros and cons of completing this rappel. I vaguely understood that I was "on belay" – safely bound to her through a series of anchored ropes, a harness, and multiple carabeners. Afraid that I would regret having risked the rappel, and choosing to trust this experienced leader, I stepped backwards over the edge and headed down. The first step was the worst. But with each unsteady step downward, a gradual sense of safety slowly untied the massive knot of fear in my stomach. I silently chanted, "I am on belay. It is going to be OK. I am on belay."

When I reached the rocky bottom, another instructor helped me release the ropes and shout up to the top, "off belay." As relieved as I was to be independent of the ropes and finished with that seemingly treacherous descent, the sense of security I experienced while moving down that canyon carved the term "on belay" in the rock of my psyche. It occurred to me later that we are "on belay" during much of life, whether we realize it or not. When illness, abandonment, death, or other tragedies come crashing through the glass wall of life, we yearn for human and divine connections that slide under our fears with a solid foundation of security. Often we simply cannot regain any sense of steadiness alone. So people reach into our lives and offer a figurative rope of hope. And we move through the daily fog of fear or uncertainty "on belay." When nature plays a healing role, it seems our strengthening hastens. Starlit skies, a canopy of oak trees, or the sun setting in stripes of crimson and gold – it is no accident that rappelling so often occurs in the midst of natural beauty, in the company of a steady friend.

From "Inward Bound," Patricia M.B. Kitchen

For authentic friendships, for those who hold us above rough seas when we feel ourselves slipping below the surface, for comrades in faith and friends we revel with, we give great thanks, O God. Amen.

40

"Their bond is one of conviction"

"Before I formed you in the womb I knew you, and before you were born I consecrated you; I have appointed you a prophet to the nations." Then I said, "Alas, Lord God! Behold, I do not know how to speak, because I am a youth." But the Lord said to me, "Do not say, 'I am a youth,' because everywhere I send you, you shall go, and all that I command you, you shall speak. Do not be afraid of them; for I am with you to deliver you," declares the Lord.

Jeremiah 1:5-8

"Even to your old age, I shall be the same, and even to your graying years I shall bear you! I have done it, and I shall carry you; and I shall bear you, and I shall deliver you."

Isaiah 46:4

Brothers on a Solid Sea

Their eyes convey love
          and their embrace communicates trust
Their bond is one of conviction
          and refuses to give in to the strongest gale
One is wind for the other's sail
          and together they navigate through the storms
Never leaving the other's side,
          their souls are eternally united

Waves pound against their ship; the star guides them
                and leaves them with a choice
Follow or defy?
                They muster and as they discuss, the star whispers
She knows that when morning comes
                they will see freedom beyond the horizon
The star prolongs the night and embraces the sailors;
                they will never forget her love.
As the sun rises, the sailors walk toward it,
                shoulders back, chins up, forever allied.

Crawford F. Brubaker III

WHEN YOU WERE BORN you cried and the world rejoiced. Live your life in such a manner that when you die, the world cries and you rejoice.

Ancient Indian Proverb

You give us, O God, the bonds of brothers and sisters and enable us to connect in significant moments. Help us, somehow, to walk each step of our lives with integrity and intention, to not take for granted the spectrum of relationships we find in family and in significant friendships. Grant us the ability to relish the gift of life and loyalty this day and evermore. Amen.

41

"The tether between a parent and a child"

For the Lord is good;
His steadfast love endures forever,
And his faithfulness to all generations.

Psalm 100:5

My son, do not forget my teaching,
But let your heart keep my commandments;
For length of days and years of life
and abundant welfare will they give you.
Let not loyalty and faithfulness forsake you;
Bind them about your neck,
Write them on the tablet of your heart.
So you will find favor and good repute
in the sight of God and man.

Proverbs 3:1-4

I RECEIVED A LETTER from a gentleman in our congregation soon after my father's death in March of 1997. In it he quoted a passage from Mark Helprin's novel *Memoir from Antproof Case.* It addresses the kind of legacy whose richness ripples through generations. It speaks of the tether between a parent and child, of any age, of being "on belay" through parental strength and respect. It is one interpretation of a life well-lived worth considering. Helprin writes:

"I was graduated from the finest school, which is that of the love between parent and child. Though the world is constructed to serve glory, success, and strength, one loves one's parents and one's children despite their failings and weaknesses – sometimes even more on account of them. In this school you learn the measure not of power, but of love; not of victory, but of grace; not of triumph, but of forgiveness. You learn as well, and sometimes, as I did, you learn early, that love can overcome death, and that what is required of you in this is memory and devotion. Memory and devotion. To keep your love alive you must be willing to be obstinate, and irrational, and true, to fashion your entire life as a construct, a metaphor, a fiction, a device for the exercise of faith. Without this, you will live like a beast and have nothing but an aching heart. With it, your heart, though broken, will be full, and you will stay in the fight unto the very last."

Are you living at the cusp where faith touches life intimately, where risks are taken and convictions lived? At times, our convictions lie close to the hearth and the risks are small, yet vital, and personal. But sometimes they rock your world.

From "One Sneeze from Death," Patricia M.B. Kitchen

I am not sure if there is anything more valuable in all the world than a wise, loving parent. And I am not sure if there is anything more numbing than the void left where a parent could or should have been. Help us, O Lord, to revere the time allotted us with parents who still walk and laugh among us. And fill the gap of a distant, absent, or painful parent with your encompassing love. Forgive me when I want to lash out and blame; keep my spirit honest and healthy and focused upon the gift of your love. Amen.

42

"Do unto others"

Ask, and it will be given you; seek and you will find; knock, and it will be opened to you. For every one who asks receives, and he who seeks finds, and to him who knocks it will be opened. Or what man of you, if his son asks him for a loaf, will give him a stone? Or if he asks for a fish, will give him a serpent? If you then, who are evil, know how to give good gifts to your children, how much more will your Father who is in heaven give good things to those who ask him? So whatever you wish that men would do to you, do so to them; for this is the law of the prophets.
Matthew 7:7-12

THROUGH THE SCRIPTURES of seven of the world's leading religions runs a single theme, expressed in astonishingly similar form:

Brahamism: This is the sum of duty: Do naught unto others which would cause pain if done to you. (Mahabharatas: L517)

Buddhism: Hurt not others in ways that you yourself would find hurtful. (Udanavarga 5:18)

Confucianism: Is there one maxim which ought to be acted upon throughout one's whole life? Surely it is the maxim of loving-kindness: Do not unto others what you would not have them do unto you. (Analects 15:23)

Taoism: Regard your neighbor's gain as your own gain, and your neighbor's loss as your own loss. (T'as-Shang Kan-Ying P'ien)

Judaism: What is hateful to you, do not to others. That is the entire Law: all the rest is commentary. (Talmud Shabbat 31a)

Christianity: All things whatsoever ye would that others should do to you, do ye even so to them: for this is the law and the prophets. (Matthew 7:12)

Islam: No one of you is a believer until you desire for someone else that which you desire for yourself. (Sunan)

God, grant me the humility and purity of heart to treat others as I long to be treated. Only, Lord, help me to treat them even better than I would expect in return. Amen.

43

"Believing is risky –
it is business-not-as-usual"

And when Jesus returned to Capernaum after some days, it was reported that he was at home. And many were gathered together, so that there was no longer room for them, not even about the door; and he was preaching the word to them. And they came, bringing to him a paralytic carried by four men. And when they could not get near him because of the crowd, they removed the roof above him; and when they had made an opening, they let down the pallet on which the paralytic lay. And when Jesus saw their faith, he said to the paralytic, "My son, your sins are forgiven. . . . I say to you, rise, take up your pallet and go home." And he rose, and immediately took up the pallet and went out before them all; so that they were all amazed and glorified God, saying, "We never saw anything like this!"

Mark 2:1-5, 11-12

THERE IS A PLACE in the lap of mystery, where the Divine embraces us not with explanations but with a deep, sometimes scary peace. For believing is risky. It is business-not-as-usual.

Long ago in Palestine, four young men, loyal to a friend frozen by paralysis, heard that a wonder-worker named Jesus was in town and maybe, just maybe, this was their one chance to help their brother run and sing at the top of his lungs again.

So they made their way to the house where Jesus was said to be, but from fifty yards back they could see people pressed against one another, peering through the windows and crowding, four people deep, around the open door.

In spite of the discouragement that flooded the four friends as they sat down in the dust to rest, one finally looked up, unwilling to give up, and it occurred to him that if they could not get *through* the crowd they could get *above* the crowd and lower their paralyzed friend down through the flat, earthen roof.

You can imagine the ridicule that followed:

> Be realistic!
> It would be rude.
> They will be *angry.*
> Jesus might reject him altogether.
> You can't dig through the roof of someone else's house.
> Dirt and clay will shower down upon their heads
>   and the roof will need repairs!
> Be realistic! *Be realistic!*

But the fourth friend turned and said, "He is our only hope and *he is worth the risk.*" We sense in the Gospel narrative that Jesus must have smiled with understanding upon seeing their display of faith that creatively crashed the barriers that kept their friend from his healing hands.

It was a time of turning tables. Believing often requires risk. I believe the Apostle Mark would simply say, "If those four fellows had not been willing to step out of the boundaries of convention and enter that house through the roof rather than through the front door, they would have missed their moment with Jesus and their brother would have remained a prisoner of his paralysis."

I sat for awhile last Thursday wondering how those four men felt as they lifted the last block of dirt and looked down at the surprised face of Jesus. They had set about doing their business, but not-as-usual, for their faith propelled them into the realm of risk-taking. And *there,* they met Jesus.

From "Business Not-As-Usual," Patricia M.B. Kitchen

May I never be afraid to risk, I pray. Clear the brush and thorns of self-doubt and timidity from the path before me. Then, in humility, may I be creative in carving solutions from the hardwood of the day's dilemmas. Amen.

44

"No man is an island"

With gratitude to the Louisiana Youth Seminar

Is not this the fast that I choose:
to loose the bond of wickedness,
to undo the thongs of the yoke,
to let the oppressed go free,
and to break every yoke?
Is it not to share your bread with the hungry,
And bring the homeless poor into your house;
When you see the naked, to cover him,
And not to hide yourself from your own flesh?
Then shall your light break forth like the dawn,
And your healing shall spring up speedily;
Your righteousness shall go before you,
The glory of the Lord shall be your rear guard.
Then you shall call, and the Lord will answer;
You shall cry, and he will say, Here I am.

Isaiah 58:6-9

N O MAN is an island, entire of itself; every one is a piece of the continent, a part of the main; if a clod be washed away by the sea, Europe is the less, as well as if a promontory were, as well as if a manor of thy friends or of thine own were; any one's death diminishes me, because I am involved in mankind, and therefore, never send to know for whom the bell tolls; it tolls for thee.

John Donne (1572–1631)

I hear your voice in the far distance, O God. Draw me near, I pray. I will go wherever you need me to go and serve those most in need. I just am not sure when, or how, or where, and some days I am unsure of why. But I know that I am yours and you plant your life-giving love within your people that it might sprout and feed the hearts of others. Lead me, I pray, whether it be near or very, very far. Amen.

45

"The value of comradeship"

Behold my servant, whom I uphold,
my chosen, in whom my soul delights;
I have put my spirit upon him,
he will bring forth justice to the nations.
He will not cry or lift up his voice,
or make it heard in the street;
A bruised reed he will not break,
and a dimly burning wick he will not quench;
He will not fail or be discouraged
'til he has established justice in the earth;
And the coastlands wait for his law.
Thus says God, the Lord,
who created the heavens and stretched them out,
Who spread forth the earth and what comes from it,
who gives breath to the people upon it
And spirit to those who walk in it.

Isaiah 42:1-5

WAS IT WORTHWHILE? For us who took part in the venture, it was so beyond doubt. We have shared a high endeavor; we have witnessed scenes of beauty and grandeur; we have built up a lasting comradeship among ourselves and we have seen the fruits of that comradeship ripen into achievement. We shall not forget those moments of great living upon that mountain.

The story of the ascent of Everest is one of teamwork. If there is a deeper and more lasting message behind our venture than the mere passing sensation of a physical feat, I believe this to be the value of comradeship and the many virtues which combine to create it. Comradeship, regardless of race or creed, is forged among high mountains, through the difficulties and dangers to which they expose those who aspire to climb them, the need to combine the efforts to attain their goal, the thrills of a great adventure shared together.

And who of others? Was it worthwhile for them, too? I believe it may have been, if it is accepted that there is a need for adventure in the world we live in and provided too, that it is realized that adventure can be found in many spheres, not merely upon a mountain, and not necessarily physically. Ultimately, the justification for climbing Everest – if any justification is needed – will lie in the seeking of their "Everests" by others, stimulated by this event as we were inspired by others before us.

I believe that we cannot avoid the challenge of other giants. Mountains scarcely lower than Everest itself are still "there," as Mallory said. They beckon us, and we cannot rest until we have met their challenge, too.

And there are many other opportunities for adventure, whether they be sought among the hills, in the air, upon the sea, in the bowels of the earth, or on the ocean bed; and there is always the moon to reach. There is no height, no depth, that the spirit of a person, guided by a higher Spirit, cannot attain.

From *The Conquest of Everest* by Sir John Hunt (1910–1998)

"Guide me, O, Thou Great Jehovah,
Pilgrim through this barren land;
I am weak, but Thou art mighty;
Hold me with Thy powerful hand . . ." Amen.

46

"Mental rest as well as physical rest"

*O taste and see that the Lord is good; happy are those who
take refuge in him. . . .
The young lions suffer want and hunger, but those who
seek the Lord lack no good thing.*
Psalm 34:8, 10

The Pulley

When God at first made man,
Having a glass of blessings standing by,
"Let us," said he, "pour on him all we can:
Let the world's riches, which dispersed lie,
Contract into a span."

So strength first made a way;
Then beauty flowed, then wisdom, honour, pleasure;
When almost all was out, God made a stay,
Perceiving that, alone of all his treasure,
Rest in the bottom lay.

"For if I should," said he,
"Bestow this jewel also on my creature,
He would adore my gifts instead of me,
And rest in Nature, not the God of nature:
So both should losers be.

"Yet let him keep the rest,
But keep them with repining restlessness;
Let him be rich and weary, that at least,
If goodness lead him not, yet weariness
May toss him to my breast."

George Herbert (1593–1633)

You are the source of my daily strength, O Lord, and your sure Presence is a daily anchor as work and studies crowd my mind. Keep me centered upon that which is strong and holy, I pray. When sleep pricks my eyes, grant me mental rest as well as physical rest, I pray. Amen.

47

"They shall not hurt or destroy in all my holy mountain"

The wolf shall dwell with the lamb,
And the leopard shall lie down with the kid,
And the calf and the lion and the fatling together,
And a little child shall lead them.
The cow and the bear shall feed;
Their young shall lie down together;
And the lion shall eat straw like the ox.
The sucking child shall play over the hole of the asp,
And the weaned child shall put his hand on the adder's den.
They shall not hurt or destroy in all my holy mountain;
For the earth shall be full of the knowledge of the Lord
As the waters cover the sea.

Isaiah 11:6-9

Jerusalem

And did those feet in ancient time
Walk upon England's mountains green?
And was the holy Lamb of God
On England's pleasant pastures seen?

And did the Countenance Divine
Shine forth upon our clouded hills?
And was Jerusalem builded here

Among these dark Satanic Mills?

Bring me my Bow of burning gold!
Bring me my Arrows of desire!
Bring me my Spear! O Clouds, unfold!
Bring me my Chariot of fire!

I will not cease from Mental Fight,
Nor shall my Sword sleep in my hand,
Till we have built Jerusalem
In England's green and pleasant land.
William Blake (1757–1827)

Grant us eyes to see similarities in the human spirit, O God. Give us the language required to speak peace. Enable us to weave creative cords which bind the riches of differing religions rather than strangling ourselves with the ropes of division. Be our sun, O God, as the planets of denominations and religions humbly revolve around you. Shed light upon our souls that we may see the unity at our roots and grow strong upon such holy ground. Amen.

PART VI

Starry Nights

48

"The woods are lovely, dark and deep"

For as the rain and the snow come down from heaven, and do not return there without watering the earth, and making it bear and sprout, and furnishing seed to the sower and bread to the eater; so shall My word be which goes forth from My mouth; it shall not return to Me empty.
Isaiah 55:10-11

Stopping By Woods On A Snowy Evening

Whose woods these are I think I know.
His house is in the village though;
He will not see me stopping here
To watch his woods fill up with snow.

My little horse must think it queer
To stop without a farmhouse near
Between the woods and frozen lake
The darkest evening of the year.

He gives his harness bells a shake
To ask if there is some mistake.
The only other sound's the sweep
Of easy wind and downy flake.

The woods are lovely, dark and deep.
But I have promises to keep,

And miles to go before I sleep,
And miles to go before I sleep.

Dust of Snow

The way a crow
Shook down on me
The dust of snow
From a hemlock tree

Has given my heart
A change of mood
And saved some part
Of a day I had rued.

Both poems by Robert Frost (1874–1963)

When days are gray and nights are cold, whether outside our windows or within our souls, be the fire of our
lives, we pray. Help us to see Thy Spirit in the wild,
whistling wind and in the stillness of freshly-fallen snow.
May the temperature of our souls be commensurate with
Thy love for us. Amen.

49

"Simple pleasures"

Vanity of vanities, says the Preacher, vanity of vanities!
*   All is vanity.*
What does man gain by all the toil
*   at which he toils under the sun?*
A generation goes, and a generation comes,
But the earth remains for ever.
The sun rises and the sun goes down,
And hastens to the place where it rises.
The wind blows to the south, and goes round to the north;
Round and round goes the wind,
And on its circuits the wind returns.
All streams run to the sea, but the sea is not full;
To the place where the streams flow, There they flow again...
*   there is nothing new under the sun.*

Ecclesiastes 1:1-7, 9

"AND YOU REALLY LIVE by the river? What a jolly life."

"By it and with it and on it and in it," said Rat. "It's brother and sister to me and aunts, and company, food and drink. . . . It's my world and I don't want any other. What it hasn't got is not worth having, and what it doesn't know is not worth knowing. Lord! the times we've had together! Whether in winter or summer, spring or autumn, it's always got its fun and its excitements."

From *The Wind in the Willows* by Kenneth Grahame (1859–1932)

The joy that swells within a heart captivated by the love of God is great, and grows greater when fed by the comradeship of others. O Lord, may I never take for granted the simple pleasures of a day. Amen.

50

"The silence of forgetfulness"

Where were you when I laid the foundation of the earth?
Tell me, if you have understanding.
Who determined its measurements — surely you know!
Or who stretched the line upon it?
On what were its bases sunk,
Or who laid its cornerstone,
When the morning stars sang together,
And all the sons of God shouted for joy?
Job 38:4-7

The Lord builds up Jerusalem; he gathers the outcasts of Israel.
He heals the brokenhearted, and binds up their wounds.
He determines the number of the stars,
*   he gives to all of them their names.*
Great is our Lord, and abundant in power;
*   his understanding is beyond measure.*
Psalm 147:2-5

O give thanks to the God of gods,
*   for his steadfast love endures for ever. . . .*
To him who made the great lights,
*   for his steadfast love endures for ever;*
The sun to rule over the day,
*   for his steadfast love endures for ever;*

The moon and stars to rule over the night,
for his steadfast love endures for ever.
Psalm 136:2, 7-9

I N THIS MODERN age, very little remains that is real. Night has been banished, so have the cold, the wind, and the stars. They have all been neutralized: the rhythm of life itself is obscured. Everything goes so fast and makes so much noise, and we hurry by without heeding the grass by the roadside, its color, its smell, and the way it shimmers when the wind caresses it. What a strange encounter then is that between us and the high places of our planet! Up there, we are surrounded by the silence of forgetfulness. . . .

After the hard, acrobatic effort of the climb, [the climber] is lost – like the poet – in contemplation; but to a greater degree than the poet, the climber can be a part of the hills around. One who bivouacs becomes one with the mountain. On a bed of stone, leaning against the great wall, facing empty space which has become a friend, one watches the sun fade over the horizon on the left, while on the right the sky spreads its mantle of stars. At first the climber is wakeful; then, if possible, sleeps; then wakes, watches the stars and sleeps again; then, at last, stays awake and watches. On the right the sun will return, having made its great voyage below this shield of scattered diamonds.

The person who climbs only in good weather, starting from huts and never bivouacking, appreciates the splendor of the mountains but not their mystery, the dark of their night, the depth of their sky above. . . . How much has been missed! . . . We should brush nothing aside, set no restrictions. We should experience hunger and thirst, be able to go fast, but also know how to go slowly and contemplate.

From *Starlight and Storm: The Conquest of the Great North Faces of the Alps* by Gaston Rebuffat (1921–1985)

In the stillness of morning, as my wet footprints make a path toward the morning paper, I hear your call in the early song of a whippoorwill. As the day accelerates, steer me away from unnecessary banter and busy-ness into a rhythm of meaning and, where needed, action. But in this quiet hour, help me to focus upon the promised peace that passes all understanding. When I am longing for the mountains of summer, help me to find the woods within me. When I yearn to smell the ocean's salty breath, help me to close my eyes and sense a growing sea of peace within me. When I shy away from new ventures and worry about ice and snow when there is still green upon the ground, help me to laugh at my own timidity, to roar and surge forth, to enter the divine realm of the forest of God . . . and there, to meet you face to face. Amen.

51

"Books in running brooks, sermons in stones, and good in everything"

"For you shall go out in joy, and be led forth in peace;
the mountains and the hills before you
shall break forth into singing,
and all the trees of the field shall clap their hands.
Instead of the thorn shall come up the cypress;
instead of the brier shall come up the myrtle;
And it shall be to the Lord for a memorial,
for an everlasting sign which shall not be cut off."
Isaiah 55:12-13

ARE NOT these woods
More free from peril than the envious court?
Here feel we but the penalty of Adam,
The seasons' difference; and the icy fang
And churlish chiding of the winter's wind,
Which, when it bites and blows upon my body,
Even 'til I shrink with cold, I smile and say
"This is no flattery; these are counsellors
That feelingly persuade me what I am."
Sweet are the uses of adversity
Which like the toad, ugly and venomous,
Wears yet a precious jewel in its head;

And this our life exempt from public haunt,
Finds tongues in trees, books in running brooks,
Sermons in stones, and good in everything.

From *As You Like It* by William Shakespeare (1564–1616)

O God, architect of the universe, artist of cypress trees, weeping willows, and grand old oaks, rivet my attention to the details of the world just outside my door. Slow me down that I may stoop to see what grows along the path to my very mailbox. Routine robs me of wonder; slow me down, stretch wide my jaded eyes, help me to revel in your created kingdom. And then empower me to restore and respect the environment which envelops us. Amen.

52

"The pace of nature"

The heavens are telling the glory of God;
            and the firmament proclaims his handiwork.
Day to day pours forth speech,
            and night to night declares knowledge.
There is no speech, nor are there words;
            their voice is not heard;
Yet their voice goes out through all the earth,
            and their words to the end of the world.

Psalm 19:1-4

I REMEMBERED one morning when I discovered a cocoon in the bark of a tree, just as the butterfly was making a hole in the case and preparing to come out. I waited a while, but it was too long appearing and I was impatient. I bent over it and breathed on it to warm it. I warmed it as quickly as I could and the miracle began to happen before my eyes, faster than life. Its case opened, the butterfly started slowly crawling out and I shall never forget my horror when I saw how its wings were folded back and crumpled; the wretched butterfly tried with its whole trembling body to unfold them. Bending over it, I tried to help it with my breath. In vain. It needed to be hatched out patiently and the unfolding of the wings should be a gradual process in the sun. Now it was too late. My breath had forced the butterfly to appear, all crumpled, before its time.

It struggled desperately and, a few seconds later, died in the palm of my hand.

That little body is, I do believe, the greatest weight I have on my conscience. For I realize today that it is a mortal sin to violate the great laws of nature. We should not hurry, we should not be impatient, but we should confidently obey the eternal rhythm.

I sat on a rock to absorb this New Year's thought. Ah, if only that little butterfly could always flutter before me to show me the way.

From *Zorba the Greek* by Nikos Kazantzakis (1883–1957)

ADOPT the pace of nature: Its secret is patience.
Ralph Waldo Emerson (1803–1882)

Help me, O Lord, to pause and admit my fascination with the dots upon a ladybug's back, and with the symmetrical lime-green sections of a caterpillar's back as he purposefully processes down an imaginary aisle upon the ground. Let me pause and see a spider web as the creative act it is (and not a sign of neglected housekeeping). Amen.

53

"The raw beauty of the world"

When I look at thy heavens, the work of thy fingers,
The moon and the stars which thou hast established;
What is man that thou art mindful of him,
And the son of man that thou dost care for him?
Psalm 8:3-4

LIKE TWO CATHEDRAL towers these stately pines
Uplift their fretted summits tipped with cones;
The arch beneath them is not built with stones,
Not Art but Nature traced these lovely lines,
And carved this graceful arabesque of vines,
No organ but the wind here sighs and moans,
No sepulchre conceals a martyr's bones,
No marble bishop on his tomb reclines.
Enter! The pavement, carpeted with leaves,
Gives back a softened echo to thy tread!
Listen! The choir is singing; all the birds,
In leafy galleries beneath the eaves,
Are singing! Listen, ere the sound be fled,
And learn there may be worship without words.
Henry Wadsworth Longfellow (1807–1882)

The raw beauty of the world stops me still, at times, O God.
But then it makes it so difficult to return, at the end of the

summer or even after a short hike, to the plastic, pre-packaged ways of a highly commercial world. Help me to find the deeper calling of nature in an ordinary walk, in a simple garden plot, in cut flowers on the table. Give me the wisdom, the words and then the will to act constructively to help fortify the natural environment. Amen.

54

"Where only wind has walked"

The earth is the Lord's and the fullness thereof,
the world and those who dwell therein;
For he has founded it upon the seas,
and established it upon the rivers.
Who shall ascend the hill of the Lord?
And who shall stand in his holy place?
He who has clean hands and a pure heart,
who does not lift up his soul to what is false,
And does not swear deceitfully.

Psalm 24:1-4

YOU SHALL ENTER the living shelter of the forest.
You shall walk where only wind has walked before.
You shall know immensity, and see continuing
the primeval forces of the world.
You shall know not one small segment
but the whole of life,
strange, miraculous, living, dying,
changing.
You shall face immortal challenges; you shall dare,
delighting to pit your skill, courage, and
wisdom against colossal facts.
You shall live, lifted up in light;
you shall move among clouds.

You shall see storms arise, and,
                drenched and deafened shall exalt in them.
You shall top a rise and behold a creation.
And you shall need the tongues of angels
                to tell what you have seen.

Tenderly now, let all of us
Turn to the earth.

From *This Is the American Earth* by Ansel Adams and Nancy Newhall

---

Lead us, Lord, in the way of purity. Enable us to look pollution, exhaust, and excess in the eye and turn the tide of environmental misuse. When we look upwards and see the Bermuda blue of the sky, inspire us to hold on to that which is natural and healthy, both within us and in the air we breathe. Amen.

55

"Choose something like a star"

And God said, "Let there be lights in the dome of the sky to separate the day from the night; and let them be for signs and for seasons and for days and years, and let them be lights in the dome of the sky to give light upon the earth." And it was so. God made the two great lights – the greater light to rule the day and the lesser light to rule the night – and the stars. God set them in the dome of the sky to give light upon the earth, to rule over the day and over the night, and to separate the light from the darkness. And God saw that it was good. And there was evening and there was morning, the fourth day.

Genesis 1:14-19

Choose Something Like a Star

> O Star (the fairest one in sight),
> We grant your loftiness the right
> To some obscurity of cloud –
> It will not do to say of night,
> Since dark is what brings out your light.
> Some mystery becomes the proud.
> But to be wholly taciturn
> In your reserve is not allowed.
> Say something to us we can learn
> By heart and when alone repeat.

Say something! And it says "I burn."
But say with what degree of heat.
Talk Fahrenheit, talk Centigrade.
Use language we can comprehend.
Tell us what elements you blend.
It gives us strangely little aid,
But does tell something in the end.
And steadfast as Keats' Eremite,
Not even stooping from its sphere,
It asks a little of us here.
It asks of us a certain height,
So when at times the mob is swayed
To carry praise or blame too far,
We may choose something like a star
To stay our minds on and be staid.

Robert Frost (1874–1963)

I look up into a charcoal sky and am awed by the patterns of light. Stars slide nightly into their eternal positions, as steady as the seasons, as bright as the sky is clean. O God, I praise you for the testimony to your magnitude as I seek out the North Star, eye the familiar Little Dipper, and locate intricate constellations. Give me pause to look up regularly and never to take for granted the grandeur of the natural world. Amen.

56

"A new perspective"

And God said, "Let the waters bring forth swarms of living creatures, and let birds fly above the earth across the dome of the sky." So God created the great sea monsters and every living creature that moves, of every kind, with which the waters swarm, and every winged bird of every kind. And God saw that it was good. God blessed them, saying, "Be fruitful and multiply and fill the waters in the seas, and let birds multiply on the earth." And there was evening and there was morning, the fifth day.

Genesis 1:20-23

I REMEMBER LOOKING out a 14th floor window in downtown Fort Worth, Texas, at noon one day. Far below people scurried across busy streets and down crowded sidewalks. They looked like the proverbial ants. Or like tiny toy people who might fit in the matchbox cars children play with. I thought to myself, "Is that what we look like through the eyes of God? Bustling about, tending to matters of consequence? Perhaps needing to rethink what matters most?" The perspective is somewhat different from far above the daily streets of our lives. The astronauts have given us proper perspective from their posts among the stars.

Is there something pressing upon your life that a *new perspective* might help ease?

Patricia M.B. Kitchen

Grant me the grace, O God, to see daily life from a new perspective. If I must lie down upon the grass to see it sideways, let it be so. If I must stand upon my head to see it upside down, give me the humor to do so. If I must close my eyes and listen more closely for a change, grant me the peace to do so. Amen.

57

"The world is too much with us"

It is he who made the earth by his power, who established the world by his wisdom, and by his understanding stretched out the heavens. When he utters his voice, there is a tumult of waters in the heavens, and he makes the mist rise from the ends of the earth. He makes lightnings for the rain, and he brings out the wind from his storehouses.
Jeremiah 10:12-13

The World Is Too Much With Us

The world is too much with us; late and soon,
Getting and spending, we lay waste our powers;
Little we see in Nature that is ours;
We have given our hearts away, to a sordid boon!
This Sea that bares her bosom to the moon,
The winds that will be howling at all hours,
And are up-gathered now like sleeping flowers,
For this, for everything, we are out of tune;
It moves us not. – Great God! I'd rather be
A Pagan suckled in a creed outworn;
So might I, standing on this pleasant lea,
Have glimpses that would make me less forlorn;
Have sight of Proteus rising from the sea;
Or hear old Triton blow his wreath'ed horn.
William Wordsworth (1770–1850)

For bugs and streaks of scarlet at sunset's hour,
       we praise you, O God.
For warm, muggy evenings, lit by fireflies,
       and icy mornings rescued by hot cocoa,
       we praise you, O God.
For rain that pelts upon the distractions of the day,
       we praise you, O God.
And for stars, celestial night-lights,
       almost a wink of good-night,
       we praise you, O God. Amen.

PART VII

Rising Convictions

58

"My bones are out of joint; my heart is like wax"

I am poured out like water, and all my bones are out of joint; my heart is like wax; it is melted within my breast; my mouth is dried up like potsherd, and my tongue sticks to my jaws; you lay me in the dust of death. . . . But you, O Lord, do not be far away! O my help, come quickly to my aid! Deliver my soul from the sword, my life from the power of the dog! Save me from the mouth of the lion! You who fear the Lord, praise him! All you offspring of Jacob, glorify him; stand in awe of him, all you offspring of Israel!
Psalm 22:14-15, 19-21, 23

Now there was a woman who had been suffering from hemorrhages for twelve years. She had endured much under many physicians, and had spent all that she had; and she was no better, but rather grew worse. She had heard about Jesus, and came up behind him in the crowd and touched his cloak, for she said, "If I but touch his clothes, I will be made well." Immediately her hemorrhage stopped; and she felt in her body that she was healed of her disease. Immediately aware that power had gone forth from him, Jesus turned about in the crowd and said, "Who touched my clothes?" And his disciples said to him, "You see the crowd pressing in on you; how can you say,

'Who touched me?' " *He looked all around to see who had done it. But the woman, knowing what had happened to her, came in fear and trembling, fell down before him, and told him the whole truth. He said to her, "Daughter, your faith has made you well; go in peace, and be healed of your disease."*

Mark 5:25-34

ONE DAY a mule fell into a dry well. There was no way to lift the mule out, so the farmer directed his boys to bury the mule in the well. But the mule refused to be buried. As the boys would throw dirt on the mule, it would simply trample the dirt. Very soon enough dirt had been thrown in that the mule simply walked out. That which was intended to bury the mule was the very means by which it rose. So don't let a few difficulties get you down. When trials begin to overcome you, use them to overcome the very thing that is trying to destroy you.

Unknown (edited)

Some days, O Lord, the dirt seems to fly upon us faster than we can trample it. Grant us courage when we fear defeat; grant us faith when impossibilities loom; grant us vision when we see only darkness; grant us optimism when naysayers surround us; grant us grace when we are tempted to groan. Amen.

59

"There is always another way out"

"O afflicted one, storm-tossed, and not comforted, behold, I will set your stones in antimony, and your foundations I will lay in sapphires. . . . In righteousness you will be established; you will be far from oppression, for you will not fear: and from terror, for it will not come near you."
Isaiah 54:11, 14

The Screams of Silence

There is *always* another way out. Stand up to them, run away.
Never give in to the wear of time, live on to see another day.
Don't just sit and melt with the bleak winter snow
Soon spring comes and everyone wants to know
What could the young boy have turned out to be?
An athlete, a star, but now no one will see.
He had a good heart and cared for all
This place got to him and he began to fall.

His parents needed to be his base;
        communication, love and trust to preside
Without them there, without their devotion,
        his soul turned to dust, blown aside
The evil percolated within his mind,
        raised its flag and declared war
Plenty of reserves on his side,
        but he did not see their love anymore.

He fought the battle himself, without the help of his friends
The last battle; fought in silence, the war came to an end
So much potential in his smile, in his eyes
The war was fought in silence, no one saw him cry.

Crawford F. Brubaker III

I feel trapped at times, O God, in the corners of others' demands. The mental boxing I engage in feels shallow and tir-
ing. Blow the winds of your eternal vision into the tight crev-
ices of my life. I long to stretch my sights and see through
your eyes. Help me, I pray. Amen.

60

"God rains the holy water of forgiveness"

Therefore thus says the Lord, who redeemed Abraham, concerning the house of Jacob: No longer shall Jacob be ashamed, no longer shall his face grow pale. For when he sees his children, the work of my hands, in his midst, they will sanctify my name; they will sanctify the Holy One of Jacob, and will stand in awe of the God of Israel. And those who err in spirit will come to understanding, and those who grumble will accept instruction.

Isaiah 29:22-24

WE DO NOT TALK about *sin* very much, do we? And that leads me to wonder if we think about it very much. We are voluble in our talk of grace, but excessively quiet about sin. The word "sinful" has slipped from our daily lexicon, replaced by more comfortable terms. We ask now if something is "ethical" or "moral." But rarely do we hear the question, "Is it sinful?" Do you suppose we think of sin as an old-fashioned word meant for tent revivals, or is it something that lurks only in dark gutters or in R–rated movies? It is mentioned 424 times in *Strong's Exhaustive Concordance of the Bible*, and we are warned of it from Adam and Eve to Jeremiah and John . . . warned that sin saps our souls dry . . . until God rains the holy water of forgiveness upon each one of us. And He does.

The odd thing is that sin is not always dressed in a black

cape. Isn't it the quiet, "pretty" sins that sneak up and whisper in our ears, that slip through the walls of our souls and settle in, making themselves comfortable within us, comfortable within our culture, and soon making us comfortable within sin itself? When sin is cloaked in reason, or in a gentle voice, or behind a closed door, or pressed deep into the drawer of our subconscious, then we don't blush. We may move through our days with a dim uneasiness, but think "it will soon pass." We become accustomed to the "low temperature of our spirits" and gradually accept it as normal.

From "They Did Not Know How to Blush," Patricia M.B. Kitchen

MORALITY IS not properly the doctrine of how we may make ourselves happy, but how we may make ourselves worthy of happiness.

Immanuel Kant (1724–1804)

Dear God, I come to you not only as a sinner, but as a hopeless sinner asking for forgiveness. Every day of my life, but more acutely now than ever, I turn my back on you and try to take control of my own life. I feel myself on a downward spiral, afraid and crying out for help, as the words stick in the back of my throat. At such a time as this, I pray for the miracle of your Presence; a Divine steadiness in my lopsided world. Amen.

61

"Many waters cannot quench love"

Set me as a seal upon your heart,
*   As a seal upon your arm;*
For love is strong as death,
*   Jealousy is cruel as the grave.*
Its flashes are flashes of fire,
*   A most vehement flame.*
Many waters cannot quench love,
*   Neither can floods drown it.*
If a man offered for love
*   All the wealth of his house,*
*   It would be utterly scorned.*

Song of Solomon 8:6-7

YEARS AGO in Robert McAfee Brown's *The Spirit of Protestantism*, I came across an illustrative analogy which I have returned to often in struggling with the difficult question of the rule of grace in the face of the apparent rule of violence and intimidation in the world. J.S. Bach's *Passacaglia* consists of a number of variations on a short theme. At first the theme is distinct and clear. As the variations unfold, the music gets more complicated, the theme is increasingly more difficult to distinguish. Soon the music seems to have no direction or purpose whatsoever. However, if you are already acquainted with the theme, you can hear it through all the apparent chaos, holding the music together, giving it direction and force. The God who preserves and accompanies us, making himself vulnerable even unto death, is also the God who is competent to meet and finally to overcome whatever this world throws at him and at us, by whose side he has graciously chosen to stand. From *The Birth of God* by John B. Rogers, Jr.

God of the Ages, and God of the here-and-now, I pray to hear the theme of your love playing through the confusion, death, and injury of the world. Sometimes I cannot help but wonder just where you are. I sense that you grieve as well, as human harm so often comes from human fallibility. Fill the holes of our hearts and our daily lives with grace, I pray. Open my ears to hear the greatness of your love, regardless of external circumstances. Amen.

62

"Nothing in the world that is alive remains unchanging"

"I came that they might have life, and might have it abundantly."
John 10:10

And I heard the voice of the Lord, saying, "Whom shall I send, and who will go for us?" Then I said, "Here am I! Send me."
Isaiah 6:8

NOTHING IN THE WORLD that is alive remains unchanging. All nature changes from day to day and minute to minute. Only the dead stop growing and are quiescent. Fresh water runs on and if you stop it, it becomes stagnant. So also it is with the life of a person.

The upshot of all such reflection is that I only have to let myself go! So I have said all my life – so I said to myself – in the far-off days of my fermenting and passionate youth. Yet I have never fully done it. The sense of it – the need of it – rolls one over at times with commanding force; it seems the formula of my salvation, of what remains to me of a future. I am in full possession of accumulated resources – I only have to use them, to insist, to persist, to do something more – to do much more than I have done. The way to do it – to affirm one's self *sur la fin* – is to strike as many notes, deep, full and rapid as one can. All life is – at any age, with all one's artistic soul the record of it – in one's picket, as it were. Go on and strike hard; have a rich and long St. Martin's summer. Try everything, do everything, render everything – be an artist, be distinguished to the last.

Henry James (1843–1916)

Dear God, lead me into the realm of humility that I may create and produce and achieve that which bears the stamp of something holy and helpful. Spare me from a suffocating ego that calls for attention and self-gratification. Show me, I pray, what good I can do today that will ease the suffering of another, build bonds where they are broken or create beauty where shadows lurk. Make me bold in my endeavors. Make me loving in my quests. Amen.

63

"It's not how long you live, but how well"

Yea, though I walk through the valley of the shadow of death,
I will fear no evil, For thou art with me,
Thy rod and thy staff, they comfort me . . .
Psalm 23:4 (King James Version)

The Lord is my light and my salvation; whom shall I fear?
The Lord is the stronghold of my life; of whom shall I be afraid?
Psalm 27:1-2

A COROLLARY of preoccupation with safety is the prevention of death, apparently forever. We will do anything to add one minute, or one hour, or one month to the life of some poor being who can never be anything but a vegetable. The Christian doctrine of the infinite worth of every soul is perverted to the infinite worth of mere physical existence.

But it is not mere existence that counts. As Socrates said, anyone can extend life a little longer if willing to do or say anything. And he also said it is not how long you live, but how well that is important. Here security is a barren ideal. We need to pay attention to what is done with that security. . . . People grow through overcoming dangers and difficulties. They are not better off for being wrapped in cotton batting. Deep within us, I think we know that we need challenge and danger and the risk and hurt that will sometimes follow. "Dangerous" sports would not be as popular as they are if this were not so.

Again, mountain climbing is not the only way of dealing with an over-organized, overprotective society. But it is one good way.

From *Four Against Everest* by Woodrow Wilson Sayre

Dear God, give me a sense of abandon, I pray. In my zeal to protect and organize and analyze the world around me, give me a sense of abandon, I pray. I want to fall in love with You and thrive in Your very real Presence. I want to surrender, for just a while, the neat plans of my life, and head into the woods, off-trail, lost in your renewing love. Lead me in a life off-balance at times, muddy and sun-baked some days, lead me in a life well-lived, I pray. Amen.

64

"Trails of dry tears"

Deep calls to deep at the thunder of thy cataracts;
All thy waves and thy billows have gone over me.
By day the Lord commands his steadfast love;
and at night his song is with me,
A prayer to the God of my life.

Psalm 42:7-8

Thou dost keep him in perfect peace,
whose mind is stayed on thee,
because he trusts in thee.
Trust in the Lord for ever,
for the Lord God is an everlasting rock.

Isaiah 26:3-4

Down the Path of Death

Ominous shadows dance around the room,
the chant of memories playing in the background
Around the fire they dance, another night,
another victim, they are uncompromising
Sweeping in like rain on a picnic, it gives no warning
and then strikes without mercy
Enveloping time, stealing it while his guard is down
and using it for iniquity
Is it fair? The epicenter shifts over time,
leaving friends and family unbalanced

The slippery slope of death,
        then trails of dry tears and parched emotion
Trails converging in a dark wood;
        will even one beam of light slip through?

Crawford F. Brubaker III

SOMETHING HAS SPOKEN in the night, and told me I shall die, I know not where, saying: To lose the earth you know, for greater knowing; to lose the life you have, for greater life; to leave the friends you loved, for greater loving; to find a land more kind than home, more large than earth.

From *You Can't Go Home Again* by Thomas Wolfe (1900–1938)

Dear God, I pray that my life can be a prayer for you. In my living and in my dying, may my actions speak declarative sentences of Divine love. We do not know when we shall slip under the sheets of death, but help me to do so wrapped in a blanket of courage, on a bed of hope, covered with the quilt of a life lived in whimsical designs. Help me when I take life too seriously. Spare me when I do not take it seriously enough. But more than anything, I pray, fill me with a fervor for living. Amen.

65

"To strive, to seek, to find, and not to yield"

Do you not know that in a race all the runners compete, but only one receives the prize? So run that you may obtain it. Every athlete exercises self-control in all things. They do it to receive a perishable wreath, but we an imperishable. Well, I do not run aimlessly, I do not box as one beating the air; but I pommel my body and subdue it, lest after preaching to others I myself should be disqualified.

I Corinthians 9:24-27

Therefore, since we are surrounded by so great a cloud of witnesses, let us also lay aside every weight, and sin which clings so closely, and let us run with perseverance the race that is set before us.

Hebrews 12:1

THO' MUCH is taken, much abides; and tho'
We are not now that strength which in old days
Moved earth and heaven; that which we are, we are;
One equal temper of heroic hearts
Made weak by time and fate, but strong in will
To strive, to seek, to find, and not to yield.

From "Ulysses" by Alfred, Lord Tennyson (1809–1892)

O God of Patriots and Heroes, of Artists, Poets, and Physicists, lift my eyes to the horizon of your great hope for humankind. Let me not be discouraged by a lack of clout or simple station in life, but rather lift me on the wings of your will which carries both princes and paupers to mountaintops of creative service. Let me not hang back or hide when the hail of skepticism or criticism falls upon me. I yearn to be of some holy use. I want to help sculpt a just society. But it would be easier to go inside and turn on the TV. Cleanse me. Empower me. Lead me, I pray. Amen.

66

"Daring greatly, spend themselves in a worthy cause"

Then the king commanded, and Daniel was brought and cast into the den of lions. The king said to Daniel, "May your God, whom you serve continually, deliver you!" And a stone was brought and laid upon the mouth of the den, and the king sealed it with his own signet and with the signet of his lords, that nothing might be changed concerning Daniel. Then the king went to his palace, and spent the night fasting; no diversions were brought to him, and sleep fled from him. Then, at break of day, the king arose and went in haste to the den of lions. When he came near to the den where Daniel was, he cried out in a tone of anguish and said to Daniel, "O Daniel, servant of the living God, has your God, whom you serve continually, been able to deliver you from the lions?" Then Daniel said to the king, "O king, live for ever! My God sent his angel and shut the lions' mouths, and they have not hurt me, because I was found blameless before him; and also before you, O king, I have done no wrong."

Daniel 6:16-22

IT IS NOT the critic who counts. Not the person who points out where the strong stumbled or where the doers of great deeds could have done them better. The credit belongs to those who are actually in the arena. Whose faces are marred by dust and sweat and blood. Who strive valiantly, who err and come up short again and again. And who, while daring greatly, spend themselves in a worthy cause so that their place may not be among those cold and timid souls who know neither victory nor defeat.

Theodore Roosevelt (1858–1919)

For courage when peering into the eyes of lions,
I praise you, O God.
For risk-taking when uncertainty looms just ahead;
For believing when crowds wail and sneer;
For moving onward
        when my feet crave the comfort of familiarity,
I praise you, O God. Amen

67

"We shall not cease from exploration"

Listen to me in silence, O coastlands: let the peoples renew
their strength; let them approach, then let them speak. . . .
Who stirred up one from the east whom victory meets at
every step? . . . Who has performed and done this, calling
the generations from the beginning? I, the Lord, the first,
and with the last; I am He.

Isaiah 41:1, 4

ON JUNE 17, 1744, the commissioners from Maryland
and Virginia negotiated a treaty with the Indians of the
Six Nations at Lancaster, Pennsylvania. The Indians were in-
vited to send boys to William and Mary College. The next day
they declined the offer as follows:

"We know that you highly esteem the kind of learning taught
in those colleges, and that the Maintenance of our young men,
while with you, would be very expensive to you. We are con-
vinced that you mean to do us Good by your Proposal; and
we thank you heartily. But you who are wise must know that
different Nations have different Conceptions of things and
you will therefore not take it amiss, if our Ideas of this kind of
Education happen not to be the same as yours. We have had
some Experience in it. Several of our young People were for-
merly brought up at the Colleges of the Northern Provinces;
they were instructed in all your Sciences; but when they came

back to us, they were bad Runners, ignorant of every means of living in the woods . . . neither fit for Hunters, Warriors, nor Counsellors, they were totally good for nothing.

We are, however, not the less oblig'd by your kind offer, tho' we decline accepting it; and to show our grateful Sense of it, if the Gentlemen of Virginia will send us a Dozen of their Sons, we will take Care of their Education, instruct them in all we know, and make Men of them.

Unknown

WE SHALL not cease from exploration
And the end of all our exploring
Will be to arrive where we started
And know the place for the first time.

From "Little Gidding" by T.S. Eliot (1888–1965)

Guide me down paths unexplored, I pray. Take any timidity from me this day and light a spark of curiosity where tepid thoughts dwell. What a gift the human mind is and I so often take it for granted. Stir my brain cells and awaken me to the conundrums around me. Instill in me a sense of purpose and discipline, layered with wonder and delight in learning. Amen.

68

"Part God, part guts"

And David said to Saul, "Let no man's heart fail because of him; your servant will go and fight with this Philistine." And Saul said to David, "You are not able to go against this Philistine to fight with him; for you are but a youth, and he has been a man of war from his youth." But David said to Saul, "Your servant used to keep sheep for his father; and when there came a lion, or a bear, and took a lamb from the flock, I went after him and smote him and delivered it out of his mouth; and if he arose against me, I caught him by his beard, and smote him and killed him . . . The Lord who delivered me from the paw of the lion and from the paw of the bear, will deliver me from the hand of this Philistine."

When the Philistine arose and came and drew near to meet David, David ran quickly toward the battle line to meet the Philistine. And David put his hand in his bag and took out a stone, and slung it, and struck the Philistine on his forehead; the stone sank into his forehead, and he fell on his face to the ground.

I Samuel 17:32-35, 37, 48-49

BRYCE COURTENAY, in his compelling novel *The Power of One*, has created a young character, small in stature yet mammoth in his dreams and determination. He is a white South African boy named Peekay who dreamed of becoming the welterweight boxing champion of the world. The novel is set in the 1930s, and near the beginning of the story, Peekay finds himself temporarily lost in a sea of ridicule and racism in a South African boarding school. Isolation and abandonment lace his young years until two adult friends slowly help raise the sails of confidence within him, allowing the winds of courage to blow through his lonely life. For Peekay, it is the gradual discovery of what is called "the power of one."

One wise friend, a scientist and concert pianist, counsels Peekay: " *Ja*, Peekay, always in life an idea starts small, it is only a sapling idea, but the vines will come and they will try to choke your idea so it cannot grow, and it will die, and you will never know you had a big idea, an idea so big it could have grown thirty meters through the dark canopy of leaves and touched the face of the sky.' " Doc looks at Peekay with his piercing blue eyes and continues, " 'The vines are people who are afraid of originality, of new thinking. Many people you encounter will be vines and when you are a young plant they are very dangerous. . . . Always listen to yourself, Peekay. It is better to be wrong than to simply follow convention. If you are wrong . . . no matter, you have learned something and you will grow stronger, but if you are *right* . . .' "

Peekay's courage rose from the power of one. In David's encounter with Goliath, his courage rose from the power of *two*. Part God. Part guts. As David departed, unarmored, for the battlefield, I suspect Saul slumped into his chair, weary, afraid, desperate, and puzzled – for this boy was not a conventional soldier. David's courage, coupled with his raw faith in God, created a new framework for the notion of an Old Testament hero and king. Were the prophets and poets of the Old Testament conventional? No. Was Jesus considered to be conventional? Not at all. So what does that mean for you and me?

From "The Power of Two," Patricia M.B. Kitchen

Lord, help me to believe that I walk in the safe shadow of your love. When I dash out into the world alarmed or afraid or unprepared, give me pause to consider the power of holiness and the depth of your Divine care. And then, only then, spur me onward, cloaked in courage born of your Holy Spirit. Amen.

69

"The essence of mountain climbing"

God is our refuge and strength,
A very present help in trouble.
Therefore we will not fear though the earth should change,
Though the mountains shake in the heart of the sea;
Though its waters roar and foam,
Though the mountains tremble with its tumult.
Psalm 46:1-3

THE TRUTH IS that part of the essence of mountain climbing is to push oneself to one's limits. Inevitably this involves risk, otherwise they would not be one's limits. This is not to say that you deliberately try something you know you can't do. But you do deliberately try something which you are not sure you can do.

From *Four Against Everest* by Woodrow Wilson Sayre

O Lord, our God, your creation is a testimony to your creativity and magnitude, and yet we know we see but a glimpse of who you truly are. Help us, when we want clear answers, to be patient. Help us, when we get frustrated by ambiguity, to learn how to wait. Help us to forge ahead into unknown, perhaps unsafe territory, for there we may see you more clearly. It is so easy to be comfortable with self-sufficiency and with that which is familiar to us. But I feel it may be time to step out of the safe frame of my daily life and into something that may be exhausting and exhilarating. It may be time to step onto a plain of living where wild winds blow and order is suspended while creative chaos stirs my soul. I pray for courage and fresh vision and determination that does not yield to bumps and scrapes along the way. Be my fresh vision, I pray. Amen.

70

"Striving for what is beyond our grasp"

*Now faith is the assurance of things hoped for, the conviction
of things not seen.*

Hebrews 11:1

Have you not known? Have you not heard?
The Lord is the everlasting God,
The Creator of the ends of the earth.
He does not faint or grow weary,
His understanding is unsearchable.
He gives power to the faint,
And to him who has no might he increases strength.
Even youths shall faint and be weary,
And young men shall fall exhausted;
But they who wait for the Lord shall renew their strength,
They shall mount up with wings like eagles,
They shall run and not be weary,
They shall walk and not faint.

Isaiah 40:28-31

THERE HAS BEEN no time in human history when mountains and mountaineering have had so much to offer us. We need to rediscover the vast, harmonious pattern of the natural world we are a part of – the infinite complexity and variety of its myriad components, the miraculous simplicity of the whole. We need to learn again those essential qualities in our own selves which make us what we are; the energy of our bodies, the alertness of our minds; curiosity and the desire to satisfy it, fear and the will to conquer it. The mountain way may well be a way of escape – from the cities and people, from the turmoil and doubt, from the complexities and uncertainties and sorrows that thread our lives. But in the truest and most profound sense, it is an escape not from but to reality.

Over and above all else, the story of mountaineering is a story of faith and affirmation – that the high road is the good road; that there are still among us those who are willing to struggle and suffer greatly for wholly ideal ends; that security is not the be-all and end-all of living; that there are conquests to be won in the world other than over each other. The climbing of earth's heights, in itself, means little.

That we want and try to climb them means everything. For it is the ultimate wisdom of the mountains that we are never so much as we can be as when we are striving for what is beyond our grasp, and that there is no battle worth the winning save that against our own ignorance and fear.

From *Age of Mountaineering* by James Ramsey Ullman (1907–1971)

Lord, lead me down a path of daily holiness that takes me not away from reality, but toward it. Help me to redefine reality in order to distinguish more clearly what is eternal in nature and what is simply a clamoring for temporary attention. I want to have a broader vision of the world and to understand the subtleties that both bind and distinguish us as the vast people of God. But in my thoughts and then through my actions, help me to recognize the high road and then to step upon it, confident that it is more worthy of humanity. Amen.

71

"The wander-thirst that will not let me be"

Then Moses summoned Joshua and said to him in the sight of all Israel: "Be strong and bold, for you are the one who will go with this people into the land that the Lord has sworn to their ancestors to give them; and you will put them in possession of it. It is the Lord who goes before you. He will be with you; he will not fail you or forsake you. Do not fear or be dismayed."
Deuteronomy 31:7-8

Wander-Thirst

Beyond the East the sunrise, beyond the West the sea,
And East and West the wander-thirst that will not let me be;
It works in me like madness, dear, to bid me say good-bye;
For the seas call and the stars call, and oh! the call of the sky.

I know not where the white road runs, not what the blue hills are,
But a man can have the Sun for friend, and for his guide a star;
And there's no end of voyaging when once the voice is heard,
For the river calls and the road calls, and oh! the call of a bird!

Yonder the long horizon lies, and there by night and day
The old ships draw to home again, the young ships sail away;
And come I may, but go I must, and, if men ask you why,
You may put the blame on the stars and the Sun
            and the white road and the sky.

Gerald Gould (1885–1936)

Be near me, O God, as my restless yearnings spread their broad wingspan. If I need to stay put and be still, then lead me toward tasks for the betterment of humankind right where I am. . . . Lift my eyes to greater visions; prepare my hands for arduous tasks. Just do not let me be numbed by the anesthesia of pleasure. I cannot see past the bend in the road right now and the uncertainty is unsettling. I just know I cannot sit still and I wonder, are you the source of my restlessness . . . or not? Amen.

72

"If you can trust yourself"

So, now, O Israel, what does the Lord your God require of you? Only to fear the Lord your God, to walk in all his ways, to love him, to serve the Lord your God with all your heart and with all your soul, and to keep the commandments of the Lord your God and his decrees that I am commanding you today, for your own well-being. Although heaven and the heaven of heavens belong to the Lord your God, the earth with all that is in it, yet the Lord set his heart in love on your ancestors alone and chose you, their descendants after them, out of all the peoples, as it is today.
Deuteronomy 10:12-15

If –

If you can keep your head when all about you
Are losing theirs and blaming it on you,
If you can trust yourself when all men doubt you,
But make allowance for their doubting too;
If you can wait and not be tired of waiting,
Or being lied about, don't deal in lies,
Or being hated, don't give way to hating,
And yet don't look too good, nor talk too wise:

If you can dream – and not make dreams your master;
If you can think – and not make thoughts your aim;

If you can meet Triumph and Disaster
And treat those two impostors just the same;
If you can bear to hear the truth you've spoken
Twisted by knaves to make a trap for fools,
Or watch the things you gave your life to, broken,
And stoop and build 'em up with worn-out tools:

If you can make one heap of all your winnings
And risk it on one turn of pitch-and-toss,
And lose, and start again at your beginnings
And never breathe a word about your loss;
If you can force your heart and nerve and sinew
To serve your turn long after they are gone,
And so hold on when there is nothing in you
Except the will which says to them: "Hold on!"

If you can talk with crowds and keep your virtue
Or walk with Kings – nor lose the common touch,
If neither foes nor loving friends can hurt you,
If all men count with you, but none too much;
If you can fill the unforgiving minute
With sixty seconds' worth of distance run,
Yours is the Earth and everything that's in it,
And – which is more – you'll be a Man, my son!

Rudyard Kipling (1865–1936)

Make my life a pattern of purity, I pray. May it be rich in
experience, lived to its limits, held in humility, and graced
with ones greatly loved. Amen.

ACKNOWLEDGEMENTS

Our gratitude to the following:

For more information about
the North Carolina Outward Bound School,
please write, call, or e-mail:

North Carolina Outward Bound School
2582 Riceville Road
Asheville, NC 28805
1-800/438–9661 x156
info@ncobs.org